THEATRE LIBRARY ASSOCIATION

The Theatre Library Association is a non-profit organization established in 1937 to advance the interests of all those involved in collecting and preserving theatrical materials, and in utilizing those materials for purposes of scholarship. The membership is international and includes public and private institutions as well as librarians, curators, private collectors, historians, professors, theatre designers, actors, writers and all other interested persons.

The Theatre Library Association meets annually to conduct its business in the fall of each year. It presents a day of conferences and programs during the annual meeting of the American Library Association, usually in late spring or early summer.

Its publications are Broadside, *a quarterly newsletter, and* Performing Arts Resources, *an annual journal.*

It is governed by a constitution, which provides for a board of directors elected by the membership, and officers elected by the board.

THE THEATRE LIBRARY ASSOCIATION BOOK AWARDS

Two awards are presented annually for books of unusual merit and distinction in the fields served by the Association.

The George Freedley Award, *established in 1968, honors a work in the field of theatre published in the United States. Only books with subjects related to live performance will be considered. They may be biography, history or criticism.*

The Theatre Library Association Award, *established in 1973, honors a book published in the United States in the field of recorded performance, which includes motion pictures, radio and television.*

Works ineligible for both awards are textbooks; anthologies; collections of essays previously published in other sources; reprints; works on dance, ballet and opera; plays or scripts; and other works at the discretion of the jurers. Translations of significant works, other than play texts, will be considered. Entries will be judged on the basis of scholarship, readability, and general contribution of knowledge to the fields served by the Association. No galley sheets or proofs will be accepted. Books nominated for the awards must be published in the calendar year prior to the presentation of the awards and must be received no later than March 15 of the year following publication.

Nominations are to be submitted in writing to the Chairman of the Book Awards Committee, in care of the Theatre Library Association, 111 Amsterdam Avenue, New York, N.Y. 10023.

The 1978 George Freedley Award was presented to The Shows of London: A Panoramic History of Exhibitions, 1600 — 1862 *by Richard D. Altick (Harvard University Press). A* Special Freedley Award Citation *was presented to* A Biographical Dictionary of Actors, Actresses, Musicians, Dancers, Managers, and Other Stage Personnel in London, 1660 — 1800, *by Philip H. Highfill, Jr., Kalman A. Burnim, and Edward A. Langhans (Southern Illinois University Press).*

The 1978 Theatre Library Association Award was presented to The War, the West and the Wilderness *by Kevin Brownlow (Alfred Knopf).*

PERFORMING ARTS RESOURCES

Edited by Mary C. Henderson
with the assistance of Wendy Warnken

VOLUME FIVE

Guest Editor: William W. Appleton

Published by the Theatre Library Association

The Library of Congress cataloged this serial as follows:

Performing Arts Resources
  Vols. for 1974- issued by the Theatre Library Association
  ISSN 0360-3814
  1. Performing arts — Library resources — United States —
  Periodicals. 1. Theatre Library Association
  Z6935.P46 016.7902'08 75-646287
  ISBN 0-932610-01-3

Produced by Publishing Center for Cultural Resources, NYC
Manufactured in the United States of America

TABLE OF CONTENTS

ILLUSTRATIONS

PERFORMING ARTS RESOURCES, *the annual publication of the Theatre Library Association, is designed to gather and disseminate scholarly articles dealing with (a) the location of resource materials relating to the theatre, film, television and radio and (b) a description, listing or evaluation of the contents of such collections, whether public or private.*

All manuscripts must be submitted cleanly typed, one side only, double-spaced and adhering to the style and method described in the MLA Style Sheet, Second Edition. Since PAR will attempt to cover a wide area, articles of extraordinary length or technical prolixity will be admissible only in rare circumstances. Photographs and illustrations may be used at the discretion of the editorial board.

Please submit manuscripts with covering letter and return postage to:

> *Dr. Mary C. Henderson*
> *Theatre Collection*
> *Museum of the City of New York*
> *Fifth Avenue at 103rd Street*
> *New York, New York 10029*

AN EDITORIAL VIEW

The avowed purpose of *Performing Arts Resources* is three-fold. First, it provides a sounding board for librarians, curators and collectors. They can write of shared problems, suggest solutions and voice opinions. Second, it informs about additions to established collections, new collections and new methodologies. Third, it gives scholars and historians a publishing vehicle for resource research.

We are about to add a fouth dimension to its purpose. With this volume, we will begin making available hitherto unpublished manuscripts, historical documents and out-of-print works which might not otherwise be published now because of their limited audience. We justify expanding the scope of *Performing Arts Resources* to encompass this added purpose by simply referring to the title. If the publication is to live up to its name, "resources" must also include reference matter that will augment library collections and give researchers access to rare material.

This volume is devoted in its entirety to the manuscript of a nineteenth-century English actor, O. Smith. Since it is an autobiographical fragment, it stood small chance of being accepted by a commercial publisher. But because of its content, its descriptions of famous nineteenth-century figures and insights into a fascinating and lively era in theatrical history, *Recollections of O. Smith: Comedian* deserves publication. The guest editor of the manuscript is William W. Appleton, Professor Emeritus of English and Dramatic Literature of Columbia University. How he came by the manuscript and his own particular interest in it are described in his foreword. Pennyplains from his collection and tinsels from the Oscar Serlin Collection of the Museum of the City of New York, many of which have never been published, provide visual emphasis for the text.

We hope the publication of this manuscript will stimulate the submission of other noteworthy and publishable historical documents. Out-of-print materials that merit attention will also be given serious consideration.

Performing Arts Resources Volume 6 will revert to the usual format and will be devoted to newly established collections or significant additions to standing collections. Submissions to this volume are warmly welcomed.

New York, 1979   Mary C. Henderson

Recollections of
O. Smith: Comedian

During a period of fifty years
in the profession

Mr. O. Smith as the Bottle Imp. The New York Public Library, Performing Arts Research Center.

FOREWORD

Richard John Smith, better known as O. Smith, has aptly been called the Boris Karloff of the nineteenth century. Tall, gaunt, with a sepulchral voice, he made his reputation playing demons, devils, monsters and assassins. As Frank Rahill has described him in *The World of Melodrama* (University Park: Pennsylvania University Press, 1967):

> Atrocities were his ordinary occupation. As Jonathan Wild in *Jack Sheppard* he hacked the fingers from the hand of Trenchard, his accomplice, sending that nobleman plunging to his doom to the accompaniment of the famous tag line, "You have a long journey before you, Sir Roland"; as Guy Fawkes he plotted with the foreign foe to blow up king and parliament; as the monster, he crushed a child to death in *Frankenstein*.

Like his twentieth-century brother-in-villainy, offstage he was the mildest of men. He was courteous, well-read, and had a talent for watercolors. He was also a passionate bibliophile who for years collected theatrical books and drawings and cherished the hope of writing a history of the stage. By 1829 he had advanced far enough with this project to induce a publisher to print a prospectus, but the history was never written, and twenty-four volumes of theatrical scrapbooks, now in the British Museum, are all that remain of his unrealized ambition. Also unrealized was his hope to write a history of costume. The chief reason for the failure of both these projects was his engagement in 1829 as a member of the Adelphi theatrical company. For twenty-five years he reigned there as master of menace. It left him little time for writing, although he did complete an account of a trip to the Continent in 1837 and eight chapters of an autobiography. The manuscript account of his trip was sold at the auction of his library in 1855, but subsequently disappeared. He also kept a diary, but this too is apparently lost, though a few scattered sheets of it have survived among his *Recollections*.

In writing these memoirs Smith evidently relied on his scrapbooks and his diary, but the extant eight chapters presented here are tentative and fragmentary. They cover his life only up to the year in which he joined the Adelphi company. Like most nineteenth-century autobiographers, Smith gives us only the briefest glimpse of his private life and he is sometimes equally reticent in writing of himself as an actor. Perhaps because he was so completely professional it did not occur to him to describe the everyday routine of an actor's life. Some innate modesty also may have inhibited him. He makes no allusion, for example, to his successful melodrama, *Lolonois* (1818). Similarly, although he gives us an amusing account of his juvenile performance as Obi, or Three-fingered Jack, he tells us nothing of his adult triumph in the same role — the role which led to his being called O. Smith. Nor does he give us any discussion of his character interpretations, though it is evident from contemporary accounts that he had a keen eye for stage effect and an artist's interest in the fine details of costume and makeup.

In the discursive manner of his day, Smith often pads his narrative with extensive quotations describing contemporary actors and events, but since these insertions are familiar and available elsewhere, I have eliminated them in almost every case. I have taken the additional liberty of occasionally correcting his dates where necessary and reordering the text. The major portion of the manuscript is written in a firm, beautifully legible hand, but it is clearly only a draft. The author's subsequent notes and additions, written in a quavering hand, make it plain that he himself recognized the need for such revisions. In the text that follows, editorial emendations and insertions are enclosed by brackets while Smith's own commentary is enclosed by parentheses.

Smith's account of his apprenticeship in the theatre spans English theatre history from the age of the Kembles to the age of Edmund Kean. During the last decade of the eighteenth century, the vast family of Roger Kemble, a touring actor-manager, established themselves as the royal family of the stage. Bred from infancy to the hardships and disciplines of provincial repertory, they graduated to the grandeurs of London where they set the style for a generation of actors. Rejecting the easy, natural manner of David Garrick, they returned to the more formal style of an earlier age. With their patrician profiles, majestic presence, and booming delivery they dominated even the vast expanses of Drury Lane and Covent Garden. Though not a follower of the Kembles, Smith appreciated their talents, and his references to Sarah Siddons — in particular his account of coming upon her, alone, in her dressing-room — are genuinely moving.

Smith also gives us telling glimpses of the theatre during the confused first decade of the nineteenth century. The Kembles were still admired, but the public was increasingly drawn to more exotic performers. They flocked to see Robert ("Romeo") Coates, The Amateur of Fashion, whose ineptitude and diamond shoe-buckles insured packed houses. Still more freakish was the vogue for child actors. The London debut of the thirteen-year-old William Henry ("Master Betty") West caused a sensation, judging from the profusion of Betty snuff boxes, prints, and medallions which have survived. In his wake followed a school of "infant phenomena," none of whom, happily, repeated Master Betty's success.

Smith's *Recollections* give us a glimpse not only of Romeo Coates and Master Betty, but some picture as well of the theatre during the age of Kean. Born the year after O. Smith, Edmund Kean also served his apprenticeship in the provinces, playing every kind of role and enduring poverty and neglect. In 1814 his blazing Shylock brought to an end the age of the Kembles. Kean, the doomed genius, the profligate, the Byronic hero, epitomized the romantic actor who disdained the boxes and played instead to the brawling galleries. His repertory became the standard for stock companies both in England and the United States, and his interpretations of such roles as Shylock, Richard III, and Sir Giles Overreach became the touchstones for judging an actor. Smith does not tell us much about Kean — he tells us more about George Frederick Cooke, Kean's only real rival — but this was perhaps because Kean was so well-known a figure. Like him, Smith made his reputation as an actor of melodrama, and like him he was not afraid of strong effects.

To get some impression of Smith's powers we must look beyond the *Recollections*. Until 1829 Smith was overshadowed by T.P. Cooke, a rival villain, but during his years at the Adelphi Smith established himself as the leading stage menace. His chilling laugh and mastery of stage makeup inspired a host of imitators. So great a favorite was he with the Adelphi patrons that when a play contained no role for him it was necessary to invent one. John Buckstone's *The Last Days of Pompeii* offers a case in point. Since the villain was obviously the volcano, Smith was pressed into service as The Witch of Vesuvius. In the eyes of his admirers he could play anything human, or, better still, non-human. His style was broad, but he performed with an assurance and ferocity that often produced shattering effects. Barton Baker describes a Smith scene in *History of the London Stage* (London: Allen, 1889):

> In one of the old dramas, I believe it was *Peter Bell,* he played the part of a drunkard, and in one scene he had to upset a cup of liquor; with a cry of horror he cast himself upon the stage and ravenously licked up the spilled drink. It was one of those daring bits of business that only a strong actor, confident in his own power, would have dared attempt; had it been weakly done it would have raised a laugh; as he did it, it sent a shudder through the house.

Associated with Madame Celeste during his later years at the Adelphi, he created key roles in two of the most long lived melodramas, *The Green Bushes* and *The Flowers of the Forest* by John Buckstone. When Buckstone dedicated *Isabelle* to Smith, he paid him his finest tribute, acclaiming the actor "the best, most picturesque devil, pirate, and ruffian on the stage."

The Theatre Library Association is indebted to Mr. Burt Shevelove, the owner of this manuscript, for permission to publish Smith's *Recollections.*

William W. Appleton

Chapter 1st

I was born on Saturday, the 28th of January, 1786, in the ancient city of York, in the Mint-yard adjoining the Theatre. My father and mother, Walter and Henrietta Smith, were actors, under the management of the kind-hearted but eccentric Tate Wilkinson, and were both of them much respected in the York circuit for talents in their profession and respectability in private life. My mother, whose maiden name was Scrace, had previously enjoyed considerable reputation as an actress in the Dublin theatre where she first spoke "Belles have at ye all!" written by Robert Houlton, Esq. My father, who belonged to the theatre at the same time, had nearly fallen a victim to the following accident.

Last Wednesday night the audience at the Theatre Royal, Crow Street, was greatly alarmed at an accident that happened on the stage. In the fifth act of *The Orphan, or, The Unhappy Marriage*, the tragedy then performing, Polydore having urged his brother Castalio to fight, merely to save himself from the crime of self-destruction, runs on his brother's sword. This tragedy was very nearly being realized, for Mr. Smith, who played Polydore, not knowing that Mr. Reddish who performed Castalio had a sword instead of a foil, rushed on the point, which penetrated his side, and had not the sword providentially broken, the wound might have been of the most fatal consequence. Mr. Smith fell, saying that he was killed! Mr. Reddish, greatly distressed in mind, cried out, "I have killed the man, but by Heavens I had no intention." The audience were much concerned for Mr. Smith, which concern was greatly augmented from the consideration of his very amiable private character. They called out to drop the curtain and were not satisfied till Mr. Ryder came and acquainted them the wound had been examined and was not found dangerous. The tragedy ended and the farce went on, whilst everybody pitied the agitation of Mrs. Smith, late Miss Scrace, who was near being deprived of her husband, to whom she had been married not quite a month. [Source of quotation unidentified.]

When Mr. Reddish was subsequently confined in the York lunatic asylum, my father and mother, at his particular request, went to see him where they found him and another actor of the name of Dancer busily engaged in concocting a scheme for the construction of a movable theatre to be formed of tin. Mr. Reddish very sensibly and politely apologized for the accident he had formerly occasioned, and as a token of forgiveness requested he might be favored with a salute from my mother. After a little hesitation on her part, it was permitted, and taken by him with the utmost politeness and decorum. [Samuel Reddish died in the asylum on December 31, 1785.]

From Dublin my father and mother soon after removed to York where my mother made her first appearance in the character of Beatrice in *Much Ado About Nothing* and [in] an interlude called *The Young Actress.* She continued the unrivalled favorite of the York circuit till a singular accident introduced Mrs. Jordan, who, under the name of Miss Francis, made her first appearance at Leeds June 11th, 1782, in the character of Calista in *The Fair Penitent* and at the end of the tragedy sang "The Greenwood Laddie."

The extraordinary success which attended her subsequent representation of an unequalled variety of characters, her beautiful figure, the charming melody of her voice, and the joyous hilarity of her mirth soon established her as a favorite with the audience, though it must be owned, her equivocal situation and appearance, as described by Tate Wilkinson, must at first have militated against her — "destitute as she really was of habiliments, her attendants deplorable" — a mother, brother and a sister — "in a strange country, without money, friends, acquaintance, or any possibility of credit." First announced as Miss Bland, then as Miss Francis, and finally as Mrs. Jordan, how extraordinary must have been the merit which could triumph over these obstacles, particularly in a cathedral town like York, where they generally pay particular regard to the private characters of actors. No wonder that Mrs. Jordan's success very naturally gave alarm to those established favorites whose reputation and consequent subsistence depended on the undisturbed possession of a range of characters both in tragedy and comedy to which Mrs. Jordan aspired.

The effect of this sudden [recruit] into the camp, and more particularly the consequences to my mother, are thus described [by James Boaden in *Life of Mrs. Jordan*, London: Bull, 1831, vol. I, pp. 40-42]:

The fine lady in comedy of the York company at this time was Mrs. Smith, an actress of great diligence and merit, in all respects the very opposite to poor Jordan, as she was well connected, in very comfortable circumstances, happy in her husband and her friends, and in possession of the most valuable line of business in the theatre. This lady [Mrs. Smith] expected at the end of September an increase to her family, and the great object of her thoughts was to make the period before and after her confinement as short as possible, that her rival might not appear or, at least, not be seen often in any of the characters she considered her own such as Emmeline, Lady Racket, Lady Teazle, Lady Alton, Indiana and others in that cast. She therefore rendered the virgin purity of some of them rather questionable to the eye and was admonished by the manager to withdraw, since the quick study of Mrs. Jordan could at any time supply her place, at a day's notice, and it was therefore idle to inconvenience herself in her present situation. Her confinement took place on the 2nd of October, in a remarkably wet season, and on the 13th the march of the troupe was to take place from Doncaster to Sheffield. In her impatience to act soon after her delivery, she actually began to exercise herself daily, in a damp garden, that she might be able to perform the journey of eighteen miles to Sheffield. She performed the journey, it is true, but the result of her folly was a lameness in the hip, which for some time threatened serious consequences. Lame as she was, however, rather than submit to Mrs. Jordan's performing the part of Fanny in *The Clandestine Marriage*, she determined to hobble through it herself, though really as crippled as Lord Ogleby seemed, and absolutely rendered herself incapable by it of all exertion from the end of October to the middle of December.

I am sure that no reasonable person acquainted with the difficulties and anxieties attendant on the profession of the stage will think my mother to blame in this affair, but that she was rather actuated by laudable ambition to sustain her position in the public estimation. Actors well know that it is almost as difficult to retain a reputation as it is to acquire one. The mistaken policy of managers, for some slight offence or causeless dislike, may remove or gradually supersede a favorite with the public, and it is a mortifying reflection to an actor to think how soon his labors and his merits are forgotten and his place supplied in their good opinion. An actor is not longer a favorite than while he is before the public. My mother's future prospects in the profession, the subsistence of an increasing family, an honest pride in a well-earned reputation, all these considerations required a strenuous exertion on her part, and the fault, if it was one, carried a severe punishment along with it, for this lameness increased with her years, and rendered her almost a cripple for the rest of her life.

The Bath managers, Messrs. Dimond and Keasberry, having heard of my mother's reputation, offered her a more lucrative and advantageous situation than that which she held in the York circuit, and she accordingly made her first appearance in the Bath theatre Oct. 3rd, 1789, in the character of Estifania in *Rule a Wife and Have a Wife* with Mr. Dimond as Leon and Mr. Knight as Perez. For many years she sustained the principal characters in comedy and farce till the cares of an increasing family and ill health induced her to retire from the stage. She died in Edinburgh, the last day of the year 1821.

My father, happy in the opportunity of returning to his native place [Bath], was engaged to play what is technically called the heavy business, which means those parts in the drama where declamation and a respectable appearance are the essential requisites. In early life having been articled clerk in a lawyer's office, he acquired a competent knowledge of the profession, and though not possessed of sufficient means to purchase a license for practising as an attorney, his character for probity and punctuality in business induced many persons in Bath and its vicinity to employ him in their affairs. He was subsequently appointed treasurer to the theatre and held the situation with satisfaction to the managers and credit to himself to the day of his death, March 1809.

But it is now time to introduce myself to the notice of my

readers. One of my earliest recollections is that of having been carried in my father's arms to see the illuminations in honor of his Majesty George III's recovery, 23rd April, 1789. My next reminiscence is having cried for the moon, and my infantine simplicity having been deluded into a belief that I had obtained my wish, in the shape of a mother o' pearl counter. The same inclination, a little varied with regard to its object, but quite as hopeless in its accomplishment, has accompanied me throughout life, and I dare say a great many more in the world who actuated by unreasonable desires to possess things beyond their reach, have at last been obliged to sit down with a diminished or counterfeit resemblance of their wishes.

As soon as I was of age to conduct myself with becoming propriety, I was introduced upon the stage in characters suited to my juvenile appearance — the child in *Isabella*, Cupid in *The Trip to Gretna Green*, Pease-Blossom in *A Midsummer Night's Dream*, &c. but it was not till the 22nd of March 1792 that I was announced in the bills for my mother's benefit in an afterpiece of Dr. Hawkesworth's, called *Edgar and Emmeline*, as "Ariel, Master Smith, being his first appearance on the stage" (Those who remember my personations of Zamiel [*Der Freischütz*], Mephistopheles, The Bottle Imp &c. will smile at my early predilection for the supernatural.) On this occasion I perfectly well remember being dressed in a white frock and trousers, red morocco shoes, my hair curled and flowing over my shoulders, a pair of wings pinned to my back, a wreath of roses on my head, a white wand in one hand, and a stick of barley sugar (which I could not be induced to part with) in the other, making my bow to the Bath audience.

During this and the following seasons several pieces were produced on the benefit nights of the performers in which their children were introduced to the notice of the public. On the 11th of March 1794 *A Midsummer Night's Dream* was acted for the benefit of Mr. [Charles] Murray, with Oberon, Miss S. Smith, afterwards Mrs. Knight of Drury Lane Theatre; Titania, Miss Harriet Murray, afterwards Mrs. H[enry] Siddons, "being her first appearance on the stage"; Pease-Blossom, Master Smith; Mustard-Seed, Master William Murray, [subsequently] the highly respected manager of the Edinburgh Theatre. On this occasion I recollect [Murray's] sitting down under the O.P. stage-box and falling fast asleep, but during his subsequent career there was never a manager nor an actor more thoroughly awake to the best interests of his profession.

[On] Sept. 26, 1793, Mr. Elliston from the York Theatre returned to Bath, where I remember to have seen him make his first appearance in Tressel in *Richard III*. Elliston was then no 21....[He] made his reappearance [as] Romeo Sept. 26th so much improved with regard to the faults imputed to him by Tate Wilkinson that I do not think the public had ever after, during his long and successful career, occasion to find fault with him for want of "fire and levity." On the 16th of November, in the same year, he made his first attempt in a vocal character, as Captain Forrester in the farce of *Hartford Bridge*. I sat on Miss Brett's knee at the stage door to hear him sing the "Heaving of the Lead." After this he played Young Meadows in *Love in a Village*, Lionel in *Lionel and Clarissa*, Belville in *Rosina*, Cross in *No Song no Supper*, Sandy in *The Highland Reel* &c. Mr. Dimond, the manager, who had been a pupil of Garrick's, and was an excellent judge of acting, and a good actor himself, perceiving Elliston's growing merit and favouritism with the public, resigned several parts in tragedy and comedy to him: nor were his abilities confined to the regular drama, for one night when Mr. Murray was acting Don Juan in the serious pantomime of that name, he sprained his ankle in leaping from a balcony and Mr. Elliston volunteered to finish the part, which he did with such success, that he retained possession of the character and subsequently played Valentine in *Valentine and Orson* and other pantomime characters.

[Here Smith inserts a brief account of Elliston's career. He follows this with a summary account of Mrs. Glover, who appeared at Bath in 1795, and Mr. and Mrs. John Edwin, who appeared there in 1797.]

In 1799 Mrs. Siddons came down to Bath and played several of her principal characters. For the first time I saw her "in all the majesty of woe." Her fine matronly and majestic figure, the deep tones of her voice, her dignified and graceful action, the fine expression of her eye, varying from the indignant majesty of insulted Katherine, to the tenderness and pathetic softness of Belvidera, the generous indignation of Mrs. Beverly, the maternal solicitude and touching madness of Constance, or the fierce and unrelenting ambition of Lady Macbeth, struck my youthful mind with awe and astonishment, and made such an impression upon me when seen for *the first time* as a lapse of years has not been able to efface.

In 1799 it was my fortune to obtain an introduction to royalty in the following manner. When the Duke and Duchess of York were at Bath they frequently attended the theatre; on these occasions Mr. Dimond, the manager, was always ready, fully dressed to receive them, and light them to their box. One evening, not expecting his royal visitors would arrive so soon, and his attention being called to a distant part of the theatre, he placed a pair of magnificent silver candlesticks with wax lights in my hands, no one else being near to whom he could entrust them, and desired me to hold them till he returned.

During his absence the Duke and Duchess arrived, found all the doors open and no one to receive them. Hearing them coming, I was in a strange perplexity as to what I should do. My first impulse was to hide myself behind the Box-door and thrust out the candle-sticks, the candles not being lighted, at arm's length. The Duke, with his usual good humour, was much surprised and amused by his reception, and pulling aside the door to see who was concealed behind it, discovered me in a dirty pinafore and a dreadful state of confusion, for "never till that hour stood I in such a presence." The Duke laughed heartily, and passed into the box, saying in the hurried manner of his father, George III, "Ho! ha! — little boy — go and light the candles — light the candles" which, encouraged by his condescension, I should certainly have done, and carried them to him, but that I encountered the manager on my way, who learning what had happened, and no doubt jealous of my introduction to royalty, rewarded my attentions with a sound box on the ear, as a punishment for his own negligence, so I dropped the candles and ran away...

My early introduction to the stage naturally led my inclinations to the profession of an actor, and a private theatre having been opened by a school fellow of mine, in a cheese loft in Stall Street, I was induced to assume the character of Lady Randolph in the tragedy of *Douglas*, two white muslin window curtains having furnished me with a dress for the occasion. I afterwards concluded an engagement at the theatre unknown to my family, with old Brumby, the Master Carpenter, to personate one of the spectres of Blue Beard's wives at a salary 6d. per night, and often when it was thought that I was in bed and fast asleep, I dressed myself, crept down stairs, and hastened to the theatre to fulfill my engagement.

An unfortunate accident deprived me of the reputation and profit I might have derived from my performance. When the door of the Blue Chamber is opened by Fatima, which character, by the way, was played by Mrs. Mountain, the ghosts of Bluebeard's wives, represented by six boys, pass across the stage, muffled up in white sheets which are thrown over them so as to give them a headless appearance.

I was the second who passed, and encumbered by my drapery, unfortunately fell down, and those who followed, not seeing the way, fell over me, which raised a shout of laughter from the audience and totally destroyed the serious effect of the scene. It having been ascertained who was the cause of the mirth, I was discharged upon the spot.

Chapter 2d

About this time it was my misfortune to have free access to Mr. Meyler's Circulating Library in the Orange Grove, being frequently sent by my sisters to exchange volumes of novels and romances, published by that fertile source of nonsense, the Minerva Press. Having scraped acquaintance with the lads in the shop, I used to borrow and read indiscriminately all the trash that came in my way. I have said *misfortune,* for I do not know anything more likely to pervert the judgment or vitiate the taste of a youthful mind than the uncontrolled perusal of the absurd and irrational publications with which the circulating library of a fashionable watering place, at that time, was provided. I began to read with avidity books of voyages and travels, shipwrecks and disasters at sea, and accounts of "moving accidents by flood and field," and as we generally feel an inclination to imitate what we admire, I became possessed with the idea of becoming an author, and commenced writing "The Adventures of Charles Montague by Sea and Land." I commenced thus: "I was born in Ireland in the village of Blarney." Here I paused, and for some time could proceed no farther, but wandered up and down the house in a disconsolate manner, waiting for a moment of inspiration and repeating to myself, "I was born in Ireland in the village of Blarney."

On my slate, on the covers of my copy books, on every fragment of paper I could lay my hands on, was written: "I was born in Ireland in the village of Blarney." Ten times a day would my father stoop to pick up some fragment of paper on which was written, "I was born in Ireland in the village of Blarney," and peevishly exclaim, "What nonsense has the boy got into his head?" At last, in a moment of enthusiasm, I finished the story, fairly copied it out, illustrated it with maps and drawings, and was so well pleased with my performance I entertained a serious intention of going up to London and presenting it to the booksellers. So one Sunday morning I kept myself out of the way, and when the family were gone to church, packed up some clothes in a bundle and with the precious manuscript in my pocket, set out on my journey to London. I had reached the first mile stone on the road, just under Walcot Terrace, when I was stopped by a reflection which had never occurred to me before, namely, that I had no money. Ignorant of its value, as I was at the time, still I knew it to be a very necessary travelling companion. So I returned, restored my clothes to the chest of drawers in my bedroom, concealed the manuscript in my desk, and crept up into the organ loft of St. Jame's church, time enough to hear the text of the sermon and be ready with it against the family came home and secure my share of the pudding at dinner time. Upon the death of my mother this manuscript was found carefully preserved among her other papers and upon reading it after a lapse of three and twenty years I was surprised at finding that I possessed so much common sense at the time.

[On July 2, 1800, John Fawcett's "grand serious pantomime of *Obi, or Three-fingered Jack,*" with Charles Kemble in the title role, had its premiere at the Haymarket. The following winter, "models and drawings of the scenery and costumes having been sent down from London, the piece was put in active preparation at the Bath Theatre under the direction of Mr. Edwin."]

My frequent visits to the painting room enabled me to obtain the earliest intelligence of the forthcoming novelty, and being told there was a black boy, the servant to Captain Orford in the piece, suited to my peculiar abilities, I made application to Mr. Edwin who had often noticed me in the theatre and at his fencing academy, Walcot House, for a strong inclination to do mischief and a desire to obtrude myself where I had no business, to cast me in the part. My hopes received a severe check on being informed that the part had already been given to the son of the stage-manager, a remarkably steady and well-conducted youth, without any of those interesting peculiarities on which I founded my claim to notice.

Irritated and vexed at my disappointment, I determined not to yield my claims and so holding a consultation with my playfellows... we determined to act the pantomime among ourselves and divide the attraction with the theatre.

Having obtained the use of a back-kitchen [from] a lodging house keeper in Garrard's buildings, with the aid of yellow ochre, soot and whiting I painted the scenery upon brown paper. Kitchen tables, beer barrels, and knife boards supplied the machinery and platforms. Kitchen chairs for the dress circle, and washing-stools for the back seats. Candles stuck in lumps of clay served for footlights.

On the 25th of November the pantomime was produced at the theatre. Mr. Edwin played Three-fingered Jack, [with] Mr. Cunningham, Captain Orford; Mr. Evans, Quashee; Master Charlton, Tuckey; Mrs. Charles Taylor, Rosa; Miss Emery, Quashee's wife. On the 26th of the following month it was brought out at the private theatre Garrard's Buildings. The part of Three-fingered Jack, of course, I claimed for myself. Our servant maid furnished me with a bed-gown, black stockings and gloves, for which she was presented with a free admission for the season.

The young gentleman who performed the part of Captain Orford, "being his first appearance on any stage," borrowed a scarlet spencer from his sister, which with a yeomanry helmet completed his costume. In addition to his other merits, he played the fiddle "like an angel." Rosa wore a flowered dressing-gown [wound] round her waist with a blue sash, and a wreath of paper roses round her head, and "by particular desire" danced a hornpipe between the acts.

The inferior characters are not deserving notice, being left to follow their various inclinations in arranging their costume. A horse pistol was borrowed for the occasion and frequently discharged during the performance, much to the annoyance of a gouty old West-Indian who lodged in the house. The price of admission was very moderate, being only two pence each person, consequently the house, or rather the cellar, was filled at first price. The receipts of the evening, after deducting the necessary expenses of rent, brown paper, gunpowder and candles, generally furnished a supper of fried sausages and potatoes to the principal performers. To this part of the evening's entertainment there were no "free admissions," *the public press,* that is, the boy who wrote out the bills, "always excepted." By attending the rehearsals of the piece at the theatre, hid in a private box, and sometimes when the family thought I was in bed and asleep, getting up, going to the theatre, blacking my face and going on the stage with the supernumeraries, I obtained a knowledge of the business of the pantomime, which might be styled a pursuit of knowledge under difficulties.

On the first night of our performance the house was crowded to suffocation, the piece was received with thunders of applause and proved highly attractive for several nights. I was so delighted with my success that I went home in my dress, with my face blacked, and frightened the servant maid into fits who opened the door to let me in. No doubt the piece would have had a great run and would have produced several overflows, but for another *run* and an *overflow* which stopped its successful career. The nature of this accident will be best explained by a copy of the written notice which was stuck upon the cellar door, to read which the cook's pattens were in requisition the whole of the day: "The public is respectfully informed that in consequence of the overflowing of the water-butt in the next kitchen, the present entertainments are unavoidably postponed. Due notice will be given of the next representation."

Having received the common education of a day-school and being indifferently accomplished in the arts of reading, writing and arithmetic it became necessary for me to decide — or rather, that it should be decided for me — by what profession or business I was to earn a subsistence and certainly no one had ever a greater variety to choose from. 1st. Mr. Joseph Barker, a younger brother of the celebrated Thomas Barker, the painter of the Woodman, Mary the Maid of the Inn, and other well-known pictures, having accidentally seen some of my attempts at drawing, was so pleased with them that he gave me a few instructions and offered to place me under the care of a friend in London, and procure me admission to study in the Royal Academy, but this offer was declined on account of the expense attending it.

2ndly. A medical friend of the family would have taken me out to Canada and placed me in the extensive establishment of a chemist and druggist, but the distance from home and friends was thought too great and the setting out too expensive.

3rdly. Admiral Edward Turrel Smith proposed to send me on board the Hannibal, a 74 [-gun ship] then lying in Kingroad, Bristol, where I should have ranked as midshipman and have received a nautical education with the rest of the young gentlemen on board, but I was thought too young to risk the dangers of the seas.

4thly. Mr. [Thomas] French, the scene painter of the theatre, who by the bye, had been scene painter with Garrick at Drury Lane, was desirous of taking me as an apprentice, but the morals and conduct of his son [were] thought to render him a very unfit companion for my youth and innocence. So I was left to follow my own inclinations, the worst guide that a lad of 14 could possibly have, to ramble about Bath without business or pursuit, associating with all the idle and dissipated [youths] with which at that time it abounded.

After a great deal of consultation, hesitation and deliberation, it was agreed to place me in the office of a solicitor in Westgate Buildings as copying clerk [to] Mr. Thomas Cruttwell, one of a family whose names ought to be held in remembrance for respectability, kindness and liberality.

Nothing could be more opposite to my previous habits and inclinations than the monotony of a lawyer's office. Shut up in a back room, mounted on a high stool, with the edge of a desk stuck into the pit of my stomach, copying dry and dull law proceedings, with the enlivening prospect of a blank wall bounding the courtyard before me, relieved by a perspective view of a bottle rack and a dustbin, my situation became irksome to a degree. I relieved the tedium of my leisure hours by reading all the plays I could procure and committing passages in them to memory, studying the art of making fireworks, spoiling a set of prints to a history of England by attempting to colour them, making kites — I wished I could have made myself wings — cutting out faces in paper and sticking them against the window for the amusement of the servants, or in short anything but attending to the business of the office.

In 1801 George Frederick Cooke, "by the permission of the managers of Covent Garden Theatre," came down to Bath for a few nights' engagement. As he was an old acquaintance of my father's, during his stay he lodged and boarded at our house. He was kind, affable, and gentlemanly in his deportment, rose early, passed a good deal of his time in reading and taking long walks in the delightful neighborhood of Bath. He often used to attract our family around him and detain us to a late hour. Delighted by his agreeable manners and engaging conversation, it was not till some time afterwards — but let me not anticipate unpleasing recollections.

Mr. Cruttwell, the gentleman in whose services I was engaged, was a great admirer of the drama, and consequently attended the theatre every night of Cooke's performance. Like master like man, the moment his back was turned I shut up the office, posted a notice

on the door "Office open at 10" and hastened to the theatre where I
secured myself a good place behind the double drums in the orchestra
to witness the performance.

Among the earliest impressions of our youth, it is certain those
made by dramatic representations are the most durable. The sensations
excited by Cooke's acting [as] Richard III, Iago, Shylock, Sir Archy
MacSarcasm, his stout square-built figure, expansive forehead, grey
and piercing eye, loud and harsh voice, powerful and of great
compass, and emphatic delivery, so impressed themselves upon my
memory as can never be effaced while memory holds her seat. In my
opinion the great charm of Cooke's acting was his perfect self-
possession, a strong originality of conception which seemed fully to
comprehend the intentions of the dramatist with competent powers
to do justice to that conception. He gave every passage of the author
with emphatic force and meaning, without any of those sudden
shrugs and starts and groans, those sudden transitions, those forced
and unnatural readings which show the actor [to] be soliciting applause
for his own cleverness and more considerate for his own reputation
than that of the poet, so that someone has said, "Cooke's acting was
like reading Shakespeare through a magnifying glass."

How lamentable that such a genius should so far forget himself
and what he owed to his profession as to yield to the occasional
temptations of inebriety — for whatever may have been said or thought
to the contrary, Cooke was not an habitual drunkard and
would abstain from excess of every kind for months together.

One night I remember his being flustered with flowing cups
[during] the 3rd scene of the 1st act of *Richard III* [Cibber's version]
where Gloucester, no longer able to endure the taunts and reproaches
of Henry VI, draws his sword and exclaims, "I'll hear no more! Die
prophet in thy speech!" Cooke assumed such a malignant expression
of countenance and flourished his weapon in such a determined
manner that the actor who played the part of Henry VI became
alarmed for his personal safety and being naturally of a mild and
timid disposition, when Cooke made a desperate lunge at him, he
stepped on one side and having no mind to run the risk of a second
thrust more fatal than the first, quietly laid himself down and died in
peace and charity with all mankind. Cooke staggered across the
stage flourishing his sword above his head. Upon this a critic in the

gallery called out, "That's not like the Duke of Gloucester!" This aroused Cooke's indignation, and with his hat on one side and his wig awry, he advanced to the lamps and looking up into the gallery with lacklustre eyes in his bold sarcastic manner exclaimed, "That's not like a British auditor!" The audience burst into a roar of laughter and applause, mingled with some hisses, and so ended the first act.

In the 2nd where Gloucester makes love to Lady Anne, she was obliged to lend him assistance to raise him from his kneeling posture. In the 3rd, by the aid of stimulants, he recovered himself a little, and gave occasional gleams of that genius which, like the sun bursting from behind a cloud, shone out in the 4th and 5th acts, which he acted as no one else ever did or could act them.

Poor Cooke paid the usual penalty of these excesses by violent fits of illness. During his recovery from one of [these] I sat by his bed all night and administered the medicine prescribed for him. On this occasion he read me a lecture upon sobriety and temperance, which made such an impression upon me as was not without its effect in afterlife; given on a bed of sickness and exhaustion, by one whom I had seen but a few evenings before, delighting a crowded audience by his inimitable acting. "Never, my dear boy," said he, "give way to a propensity to drink. It deprives a man of his health and faculties, and injures his interests and respectability in life [and] degrades him in the eyes of the world..."[1]

The effect produced on my mind by Cooke's acting, during my frequent visits to the theatre, and the successful representation of one or two grand serious pantomimes, at that time an extraordinary novelty in the country, completely unsettled my inclinations for the dull routine of a lawyer's office. Some evil connections which I had formed, which led to a total neglect of my appointed pursuits, and an accident produced by some experiments in pyrotechnics, which destroyed several papers and parchments and nearly set the house

---

[1] Smith noted in his diary on October 31, 1837: "This evening at the Adelphi Theatre I was accosted by one of the supernumaries [sic] who paid me some very extravagant compliments on my acting to which I paid very little attention as the man seemed intoxicated. Mr. Yates shortly afterwards informed me that it was a natural son of George Frederick Cooke's, that from motives of charity he had employed him in the theatre at 1s. per night. Shortly afterwards he was compelled to discharge him for drunkenness and inattention."

Cork, proceeded from thence to Waterford, here we quarrelled and dissolved partnership. He embarked on board a vessel for America and I in one for Liverpool.

Upon our entering the Mersey, the vessel was boarded by the press-gang and those among the passengers who could not give a good account of themselves—and I am sorry to say that I was among the number—were sent on board a receiving ship in the river. Here, after having been drawn up on the quarter[-deck], we were severally questioned as to our names, business or profession. When it came to my turn I replied that I was an actor and belonged to the Liverpool company. This required confirmation and the Lieutenant [requested] a taste of my quality so I gave young Norval's speech from the play of *Douglas*, "My name is Norval," which was received with general approbation and applause from the gang—I beg pardon, I mean the auditors, and what was better still, I was liberated and set on shore. Fearful of further detention, for the *press* was very *hot* at the time, and I had no wish to be *hot pressed* [as paper is], I set off for Leeds where my sister was acting with the York company. Failing to procure an engagement, I wrote to Mr. [William] Macready, [father of the eminent tragedian, William Charles Macready], who was about to open the Sheffield Theatre with [Master Betty], the Young Roscius.

A few days later I was gratified by receiving from Mr. Macready the offer of an engagement at a salary of 15s. per week as Prompter, actor-of-all-work, to assist occasionally in the painting-room, and, in fact, to make myself "generally useful," as the saying is. I accepted the terms with pleasure and proceeded to Sheffield, where I made my first appearance as a regularly engaged actor on the same evening with Master Betty, the Young Roscius, Sept. 17, 1804. In order to conceal any nervous timidity I might be liable to on this important occasion, the character chosen for my debut was that of the trembling coward in *Douglas*....

When I came on, having a youthful appearance and being a strange face, the audience supposed me to the the attraction of the evening and received me with thunders of applause, with which I felt highly gratified, but quickly perceiving their mistake, they most unequivocally expressed their disapprobation at their own want of discernment. Rather an ominous reception for a first appearance.

Having been often questioned as to my opinion of the real merits of the Young Roscius, I will freely state my "agitation of the matter." It was natural enough for those who had never seen him to treat the accounts received with derision and skepticism. That a boy between 12 and 13 years of age should assume with success a range of tragic characters hitherto attempted only by actors of mature age, after years of application and study, seemed so utterly inconceivable that curiosity and expectation were excited to the utmost. The doors of the Sheffield Theatre were besieged at an early hour for admittance. Ladies and gentlemen were to be seen struggling for places at the expense of their bonnets, hats, shawls, coat tails, shoes and shirt frills. The Theatre at that time held little more than £100, but the price of the boxes being raised from 3s. to 4s. and the Pit from 2s. to 2s. 6d., the receipts for the 14 nights Master Betty played there amounted to £1,530. During his stay in Sheffield many families of distinction took lodgings at the hotels &c. for the whole period of his engagement, while carriages labelled: "Theatrical Coach, to carry individuals to see the Young Roscius," were stationed at Doncaster Races to take the passengers from the sports of the turf to the more rational amusements of the stage, and it was with difficulty that beds could be procured in Sheffield upon any terms.

If his youth and interesting appearance upon his entrance spoke in his favour, his uncommon self-possession and attention to the business of the stage, his originality of conception, graceful deportment, correct and energetic delivery, quickly silenced all objections. Proving however great the expectations formed of him, or the encomiums which had been bestowed upon him, he deserved the reputation he had acquired. He was, in fact, the most extraordinary instance of precocious talent the stage ever produced or perhaps ever will produce again. When not engaged in the business of the scene, his manners were modest and unassuming, always distinguished by kindness and consideration, and a natural goodness of heart which ensured him the regard and respect of everyone. These qualities have "grown with his growth" and attended him into private life. Long may he live to enjoy the reward of his talents and the affection and friendship of all who know and respect him for his amiable qualities.

Mr. Macready, my first manager, was a very proud and irritable man, but a perfect gentleman, and of the most honourable principles: at the same time, one of the most industrious and indefatigable managers I ever met with. Possessing an intimate knowledge of the profession, and all the capabilities of a theatre, with him there was nothing *impossible*. He always kept the audience and his actors on the *qui vive* with a continued succession of novelty, actors from London, new pieces and revivals. I soon [found] my 15s. a week no sinecure. Possessed of very moderate ability, and totally ignorant of the business of a theatre, Mr. Macready soon contrived to make me "generally useful." After holding the prompt book during the rehearsal of two or three pieces, I had, with the assistance of the master carpenter, to make out plots of the scenery, give a list of properties that might be wanting to the property man, write out the stage letters, and perhaps the inferior parts in the piece for the next night—books were too expensive, we had no cheap edition of plays then—and perhaps assist in the painting-room till the curtain drew up when I held the prompt book for the evening, occasionally laying it down to deliver a message, or to play the old man or the lover, in the ballet dance, which was invariably included in the evening's entertainment. This was a severe school but an admirable one for a young actor, and I may truly say what knowledge I have obtained of the stage and its arrangements, the foundation of it was laid under Mr. Macready's management.

One or two pantomime actors being engaged "from the London theatres"—how the name of London used to ring in my ears and fill me with hopes that I might one day hold a conspicuous situation there—induced me to distinguish myself in order to attract their notice. Though I was not allowed to play any part of consequence in their *grand serious pantomimes*, I determined to attract attention by my costume. My father having sent me a rough great coat for the winter, I cut it up without remorse or hesitation to make a robber's dress, and having sat up all night to ornament it with black and red worsted binding, I decorated it with a profusion of brass buttons. I then made a large pair of brown paper tops to my boots and gloves, and with a tremendous plume of cock's tail feathers, which my landlord's son remorselessly plucked from the unfortunate fowls in the neighborhood, I shone forth the admiration and envy of the rest of the band.

This love of brass buttons and tin foil made serious inroads on my finances and compelled me to walk several long journeys, which I have sometimes commenced after the performances of the evening. Mr. Macready, tired I suppose of my stupidity and negligence, had a method of accelerating my pace upon these occasions by saying, "Sir, if you are not in time for rehearsal tomorrow morning, you need not come at all, for I'll discharge you."

At the conclusion of the Sheffield season the company moved to Rochdale, and as there was no regular means of conveyance between the two towns, and I could not afford to take my share of a chaise, the mode by which most of the performers travelled, I set out early in the morning after the theatre closed to walk the journey—about 50 miles—and was nearly lost in the snow crossing Blackstone edge. The accident is detailed in the following letter to my father.

Rochdale. Feb. 1805

My dear Father:

Thank God I have reached Rochdale in safety which I assure [you] I did not expect to do on Monday last. I left Sheffield on Sunday morning at 7 o'clock, alone, and on foot, and found the road in many places cut through the snow, which was 8 or 9 feet in depth. I made my way through a cross country road to Thong, a village, about 22 miles from Sheffield, where I slept. Early the next morning I arose to pursue my journey which lay over Blackstone edge, a high range of hills, hoping to reach Marsden to breakfast. After proceeding 3 or 4 miles through a heavy fall of snow which at times prevented me from seeing three yards before me, I lost the track of the road and bewildered in my fruitless attempts to regain it, I found it impracticable to proceed or return. Weary, hungry and benumbed with the cold, I sunk down in the snow under the shelter of a projecting rock. Here I soon found a drowsy, sleepy sensation creeping over me, and an insensibility to the cold, which my early reading in voyages and travels had taught me was the forerunner of dissolution.

I took out my pocket book and endeavoured to trace a few lines to you, my dear parents, but my fingers were incapable of guiding the pencil, and I had resigned myself to my fate with indifference, when I thought I heard the barking of a dog. This aroused me from my sleep of death, and I endeavoured to attract his attention by calling out, for I was not capable of other exertion. This sagacious creature soon after found me, licked my face and hands, and by running backwards and forwards and whining and barking drew his master's attention to the place where I lay. He was on horseback, and coming to my assistance with some difficulty placed me behind him. I held fast, and the motion of the horse helped to restore the circulation of my blood. The dog ran before us, barking and yelping as if he shared in the joy of his master at having preserved the life of a fellow creature. The farmer, for such he was, carried me to his house at Marsden, where I was most kindly and hospitably treated. Obtaining a conveyance in a cart going to Rochdale, I arrived there in time enough for the evening's performance. What a contrast! In the morning nearly perishing in a snow storm, and in the evening assisting in the brilliant gaities of a theatre. I hope I shall never be so ungrateful as to forget this interposition of providence in my behalf.

Yours &c.

R. J. Smith

While the company were at Rochdale we used to play occasionally at Bolton le Moors, Mr. Williams, the scene painter, and myself being sometimes obliged to go over on the Sunday and paint the scenery that might be wanted for the Monday night's performance. Now the theatre, which had originally been a chapel, was let on Sundays to a Methodist preacher, on condition that he said nothing against the interest of the manager, or the profession of the stage. The green curtain being let down, hid the stage from the congregation who took their places in the boxes, pit, and gallery. A temporary pulpit was placed before the curtain, so that while Williams and myself were engaged in painting scenery at the back of the stage, Praise-God-Barebones was holding forth in a broad Lancashire dialect in front of it. As I could distinctly hear every word that he said,

Williams gave an occasional hint that he overheard him by a loud *Ahem!* whenever he aluded to the profession of the stage in disrespectful terms. This was a sad restraint upon his eloquence.

Being employed to assist in decorating the front of the theatre, it struck me it would produce a very pleasing effect if I were to splash the columns and pillars that supported the ceiling of the boxes so as to resemble granite. So I mixed up two pots of paint, one of light blue and the other of pink, and splashed away with great effect, without much regarding where the colour went to.

When this job was completed the effect was beautiful, and I expected to receive the thanks of the manager and the approbation of the public for my taste and judgment. Unfortunately I had forgotten to mix any size with the colour and having liberally splashed the seats and cushions in the front of the boxes at night the effect soon became visible upon the dresses, hands and arms of the company and from thence was transferred to their faces, so that when bowing to, or receiving the acknowledgements of their friends they were surprised at the ill-concealed mirth their appearance excited. When the cause was discovered they left the theatre in confusion and the next morning complaints poured into the box office, which reaching the ears of the manager, he soon ascertained the cause and would have discharged me but Williams said he could not do without me and as no other assistant [was available] I was retained with a caution to restrain my splashing propensities.

As I never professed myself to be more disinterested than the rest of the world, I was tempted by the offer of £1 per week from the Edinburgh theatre to relinquish my engagement with Mr. Macready and in January [1806] made my first appearance in *Auld Reekie* [Edinburgh]. I soon found a very agreeable change in my situation. I was engaged as an actor only, my salary was better, there were no long journeys to take, the business was conducted with more regularity and I had leisure to improve my slender ability. Urged by a laudable desire to render myself conspicuous in my profession, and forming too favourable an idea of my own capability, I arrived at the higher walk of tragedy and devoted myself to the study of many of the principal characters in Shakespeare's plays and not only the principal characters but the plays themselves, in the vain hope that I should one day or other be allowed to signalize myself by their representation.

I used to read and recite aloud upon Salisbury Crags, Arthur's Seat and the Calton Hill when they were not quite so accessible nor so well frequented as they are now and "pierce the caves where airy echo lay" with my wild ravings in *Coriolanus, Macbeth, Hamlet, King Lear,* and *Richard III.* There is no requisite more necessary for a young artist than a sincere enthusiasm, or endeavour to excel in his profession, but at the same time there is no quality more liable to render him an object of ridicule or discouragement. My assiduity and attention to my profession subjected me to the scoffs and censures of the indolent and thoughtless who merely entered the profession as a refuge from poverty and idleness and regarded my attempts at notoriety as a tacit reproach to their own indolence.

The audience too, particularly the pit, which was principally composed of young medical students, was sure to criticize me severely whenever I attempted anything serious. Perhaps it was my appearance which excited their risibility. Tall, and as thin as a greyhound, with a weak and broken voice, I overdressed and overacted what I had to do. It is very few young actors who are competent judges of their own qualifications and if left to the dictates of their vanity and ambition would quickly find a warning in the public voice. These checks that I received taught me to be content with a lower grade in the drama than my vanity had suggested and here I sometimes received the applause of the audience and the approbation of the great masters of their art. Even now I recall to my remembrance, with pride and pleasure, Mr. Cooke having said that he never heard the speech of the 1st Murderer in *Macbeth* so well spoken...[and] Mr. John Kemble remarked on hearing me speak Sr. Richard Vernon's description of the Prince of Wales, "I saw young Harry with his beaver on," "That young man will do." Or the gratifying compliment paid me by Mrs. Siddons at the rehearsal of *Henry VIII* where the messenger rudely entering the sick chamber of Queen Katherine is reproved by [Griffith] and replies:

> I humbly do entreat your Highness's pardon;
> My haste made me unmannerly. There is staying
> A gentleman sent from the king to see you.

Mrs. Siddons with that calm dignity to natural to her, and which accompanied her throughout the common occurences of life, said, "Very well."

To have been upon the same stage and to have received instruction and approbation from Kemble, Siddons, Cooke, Chas. Kemble, Young, Kean, Elliston, Fawcett and Bannister are among my most pleasing recollections.

Here I cannot help noticing the kind, considerate and gentlemanly manner in which these actors of the old school communicated their instructions to those beneath them. There was no affected air of superiority, no attempts at intimidation or efforts to crush, or keep in the background the inferior actors who strove to do their best. Such assumption they felt to be unnecessary, since everyone paid a willing homage to their talent and felt honoured by their notice.

What a different feeling has influenced several of our eminent tragedians who strove by the power which they exercised over managers, authors, and actors to intimidate and deprive of their self-confidence those with whom they were associated, endeavouring to stifle and subdue any appearance of talent which they conceived likely to divert the public attention from themselves. It was lamentable that persons so distinguished for talent and judgment, and who had it in their power to do so much for the cause of the drama should occasionally give way to such ebullitions of temper as to render what should have been a pleasing employment an ungracious task.

Chapter 4th

In 1807 I returned to Bath where I found an opening in a line of business I had never before attempted, and in which I have subsequently obtained some little reputation, the meaner villains of the drama, robbers, ruffians and assassins, a cast of character generally neglected or placed in the hands of actors unwilling or unable to do them justice. It is certainly an ungrateful and unprofitable task to represent such characters but if the stage is "to hold the mirror up to Nature" and to show Vice her own feature, I know no reason why such accessories to the effect of a drama should be neglected. The heroic villain of the stage generally possesses some redeeming quality or justifiable motive for his crimes, as revenge for injuries real or supposed, daring bravery in accomplishing projects of ambition or revenge, or by the force of superior intellect triumphing over his opponents; but for the hired ruffian, the common stabber, or the cowardly assassin there can be neither admiration nor sympathy, and the only feelings he can excite must be disgust, contempt or execration. In fact, the audience have generally thought the dénouement of any piece in which I played to be incomplete, or unsatisfactory unless I was shot, stabbed, poisoned, drowned, strangled, burnt, or led off to execution, when they have seldom failed to express their unequivocal satisfaction at my deserved punishment. The part which I am playing at this present writing [August, 1853] is a striking instance of this assertion. I am knocked down in the first scene, kicked in the second, bound and gagged in the third, and shot in the last, and all without exciting the slightest degree of compassion for my sufferings. Nay, were I to empanel a jury from among the audience to try the question, I feel convinced they would return a unanimous verdict of "serve him right!"

Unfortunately, it sometimes happens [that] this feeling of dislike for the character he represents follows the actor into private life, as I have too often experienced, and having passed so long for a villain or a rogue, it has required all my fortitude and philosophy to bear up against such [un]deserved censure, and convince my friends that I was not in reality the character I played.

During the vacation of the Bath season 1807-8 I was engaged by Mr. [Henry] Thornton or, as he was more familiarly called, Old Thornton, for the Gosport and Arundel theatres, to make myself generally useful and in the course of the season to get up a serious pantomime.

(Here let me say one word in remembrance of a species of dramatic entertainment which was at one time held in great estimation but is now extinct and lost to the stage — I mean the performance of serious pantomime. I say lost for there is as much difference between the present ballet pantomime and that which preceded it as there should be between tragedy and melodrama. I am aware that many persons have considered the performance of serious pantomime as degrading to the regular theatre, but it must be one of the principal objects of a manager to amuse the mind and interest the feelings of an audience without offense to reason or morality. I know no species of entertainment more likely to conduce to that purpose. It is not for me to attempt a display of classical knowledge by referring to ancient authorities for proofs of the estimation in which the art was formerly held; but thus far I may say. Authors of estimation have not disdained to employ their pens in its description and have recorded such facts as were in honour of the profession, describing the pantomime as, "Men whose eloquent hands had a tongue, as it were, on the lip of each finger. Men who spoke while they were silent, and who knew how to make an entire recital without opening their mouths. Men who, in short, Polyhymnia had formed in order to show there was no necessity for articulation in order to convey their thoughts." The art was very popular with the modern Italians and the French: from them it came to this country, and all the dramatic authorities speak highly of the abilities of Rich, under the name of Lun. Garrick has honored his memory in the following lines [from his prologue to *Harlequin's Invasion*]:

When Lun appear'd, with matchless art and whim
He gave the power of speech to every limb:
Tho' mask'd and mute, convey'd his quick intent
And told in frolic gestures all he meant.

Subsequently we have produced several artists in that way whose performances were little, if at all, inferior to those we read of. It is unfortunate that no description, however vivid, can convey to the mind more than a slight idea of bygone theatrical talent. Those few who may recollect the acting of M. D'Egville in *Caractacus* and Oscar Byrne in *Hengo*, M. Dubois in *Orson*, Robert Lalois in *Werter*, John Bologna in *The False Friend*, or Joe Grimaldi in *The Wild Man* will bear me out in my assertion. Where an interesting story has been chosen, such as *Oscar and Malvina, Perouse*, or *Don Juan*, aided by picturesque scenery, appropriate costume and decorations, music selected from or composed by the first musicians, and supported by the just and expressive action of the performers, I know of no entertainment more likely to attract and gratify an audience. These performances have been superseded by melodramas where the actor not requiring the accomplishments of dancing, fencing, or music, finds it much easier to express his meaning by language; or ballets, where graceful postures, elegant attitudes, feats of strength and agility, and a liberal display of the person gratifies a mixed audience who come to the theatre merely to be amused without the trouble of thinking.)

Old Thornton, manager of the Windsor, Gosport, Ryde and Arundel theatres, was one of the most singular and eccentric individuals in a profession which has produced so many extraordinary characters. The stories related of his absence of mind, and the mistakes and absurdities committed by him are innumerable. Among his other peculiarities he had great difficulty in recollecting the title of any play or farce and to assist his memory generally chose the name of some principal character or striking incident in the piece itself. For instance, he called the play of *Pizarro* "the Temple of the Sun play," *The Castle Spectre* "the old man in the cellar," and *George Barnwell* "my uncle at Camberwell," at the same time pulling and pinching his nose to stimulate his recollection.

Having stipulated in my engagement to play all the robbers and assassins I packed up my scanty wardrobe, not forgetting a pair of russet boots, a robber's hat, a black wig and a fighting sword, and proceeded to Gosport. On entering the town I was struck with astonishment to see myself announced for the next night to play Sir Lucius O'Trigger in the play of *The Rivals*, and Sir James Elliott in the farce of *The Liar*, parts that I had never played or even contemplated playing.

I hastened to the theatre and obtained an audience of the manager. I found Old Thornton seated in a gilt chair by the fireside and suffering from an attack of the gout. Dressed in an old brown great coat, tied round his waist with a military sash, a blue worsted stocking upon one leg and a red one upon the other, his hair very carefully dressed and powdered, and upon his head the crown, minus the brim, of a black velvet hat. After introducing myself, I endeavoured to convince him of my unfitness for the characters for which he had announced me, and the utter impossibility of my studying them against the next night: but he was not to be convinced by any argument I could make use of, insisting that I was engaged to make myself generally useful.

"And you know, Mr. Simpson —"

"I beg your pardon, sir, but my name is Smith."

"Yes, I know. The part of Sir Patrick O'Neale —"

"I presume you mean Sir Lucius O'Trigger."

"Yes, I know, Mr. Smithers," said he, pulling his nose. "He's a Scotchman."

"No, sir, an Irishman."

"Ah, I know very well. He beats the lawyer that's hid behind the screen in a sack — what's his name?"

"I suppose, sir, you mean Endless in *No Song no Supper*."

"Yes, yes, that's it — the shoulder of mutton farce."

"But, sir, the farce announced is *The Liar*."

"Oh, yes, I know he's a liar, but his part is none the worse for that, Mr. Sims. You must do the best you can with Major O'Flaherty in the play. We'll cut out the music to accomodate you and — Betty! let Mr. Smithson have the best blue satin shape for the part of General Elliott in the farce."

Mrs. Egerton from the Bath theatre was announced Monday, August 15th to play the part of Portia in *The Merchant of Venice* and on the evening in question all went smoothly till the 4th act when it was discovered that the person who was to have played the Duke was absent from the theatre. The stage manager was puzzled to find a substitute for the play was full of characters and the company very thin of actors. Upon consulting Old Thornton he immediately undertook the part being, as he said, perfectly well acquainted with every line of the "Jew with the scales" play. He accordingly hobbled down the stairs, and while his factotum, Betty, was dressing him in a black gown and a barrister's wig, he was rubbing his chin and eyebrows with a piece of whitening, to give him the appearance of age, though time had already set his mark upon him, and refreshing his memory by reading the trial scene from the prompt-book without any regard to distinction of character. Being fully prepared, in his own mind, he ordered the act drop to be rung up, and immediately commenced with the beautiful speech, "The quality of mercy is not strained," and would have gone through the whole of Portia's speeches before she came upon the scene. Several attempts were made to interrupt him but in vain, he replied in the words of the different characters and rambled about from Shylock to Bassanio and from Gratiano to Antonio, blending their speeches together in a most extraordinary and ludicrous manner. Poor Mrs. Egerton was driven half-distracted and after vainly entreating someone to go on and stay the torrent of his eloquence, she snatched up a letter from the prompter's place, gave it to Nerissa, and sent her on the stage to deliver it to the Duke. This brought matters to a climax and was the crowning absurdity of the scene. This letter was supposed to come from the learned Bellario at Padua and recommends the young doctor, Balthazar (Portia), to decide the cause in question between the merchant and the Jew. This letter, unfortunately, happened to be one intended for the farce of *The Deuce is in him.* This the Duke deliberately opened and read as follows:

"Dear Sister,
    The bearer of this letter is a lady whose case is truly compassionate, and whom I most earnestly recommend to your protection. Take care of her — not too many questions. I shall be in town in a few days."

He then very gravely added, perfectly unconscious of the ridicule excited, "You hear the learn'd Bellario what he writes, and here, I take it, is the lady come." After the Gosport season had terminated the company was removed to Arundel, where amongst other attractive novelties *George Barnwell* was announced. The part of the Uncle, from a motive of spite and jealousy on the part of the stage manager, was cast to Tom Herring, certainly the most unfit man in the company for the part. He was a good low comedian and singer of comic songs, and a faithful representative of a sailor, but certainly without an atom of sentiment in his composition. However, he made no objection and read the part very gravely at rehearsal, but I could perceive from his manner that some mischief was intended. At night he kept himself out of the way till his cue was given when he made his appearance in a court suit of cut velvet much too large for him, the knees of his small clothes reached to his ankles, the tail of his coat trailed upon the ground, and he wore on his head a powdered wig and a large gold laced cocked hat.

The audience were at first struck dumb with astonishment which was succeeded by shouts of laughter and applause, they supposing him to be the comic character of the piece. The stage manager who played the part of George Barnwell stood ready at the wing, waiting for his cue to stab his uncle, enraged and disconcerted beyond measure when he saw all his tragic efforts likely to be turned into ridicule. Herring was not too perfect and consequently anxious to die as soon as possible, when something like the following colloquy took place between them.

Herring: If I was a superstitious I should say — (aside to the manager) Come and kill me.

Manager (behind the scenes): I shan't till I get my cue.

Herring: Danger lurks unseen and death is nigh. (aside) Come and kill me.

Manager: This conduct is disgraceful, sir. You shall be forfeited for this.

Herring: My imagination is filled — with all sorts of things — kill me!

Manager: Go on, sir, go on. (greatly enraged)

Herring: I can't — If you don't come on and kill me, I shall kill myself.

And suiting his action to the word, he stabbed himself with the book in his hand, fell down and died with such extraordinary contortions and grimaces as convulsed the audience with laughter and put an end to that act of the tragedy. There are more ludicrous stories related of this character, the uncle in *George Barnwell*, than of any other in the drama, and why it has generally been given to actors incapable of doing it justice I cannot conceive. Certainly the soliloquy written for him is as solemn and affecting as anything I ever read. . . .

Mr. Cunningham and others of the Bath company who had passed their vacation at the Swansea Theatre, then under the management of Mr. Cherry, upon our meeting at Bath for the winter season, spoke very highly of the pantomimic abilities of a young man of the name of Kean. I find the following notice in the Bristol journal June 1809: "Lately was produced at the Swansea theatre a new grand ballet called *The Savages* under the direction of Mr. Kean." . . .

In the year 1809 when this country was threatened with a French invasion, a unanimous feeling seemed to possess all classes of society in this country, who freely proferred their services in defense of its liberty and institutions. Volunteer corps were formed in every part of the kingdom, every trade and profession was inspired with military ardor, nor were the players behind their fellow-subjects in loyalty and devotion to the common cause. (The following notice at the bottom of the Covent Garden playbill of October 29, 1803 is certainly a curiosity in theatrical annals: "The Public are most respectfully informed that the attendance of many of the performers upon military duty in the Volunteer Corps having rendered it impossible to produce the new musical drama entitled *The Wife of Two Husbands* this evening, the piece is therefore unavoidably deferred till Tuesday next.") Mr. Dimond, manager of the Bath theatre, commanded a company, and the actors very naturally fell into the ranks: even the band laid aside their instruments of harmony and took up the weapons of war. Inspired by the instances of military ardor by which I was surrounded, I joined a Rifle Corps commanded by Captain Messiter. When called out upon Field days with the rest of the volunteers, after assisting in various evolutions upon Claverton Down (it was not enclosed then) we left them to continue their marches and countermarches and scampering over hedges and ditches to the admiration and astonishment of the country bumpkins, made the best of our way to the Brass Knocker where we recruited our energies after the fatigues of war.

While performing *Permanent duty* for 14 days at Bristol, the rifle company were set to keep guard over the French prisoners at

Stapleton, about 2 miles from Bristol. The moon occasionally shining through broken clouds gave an indistinct and illusive appearance to surrounding objects. A dead silence reigned around, unbroken save by the challenge of the watchful sentinels upon the walls "in the dead waste and middle of the night." I thought I saw the tall figure of a Frenchman concealing himself under the shadow of the wall. I immediately challenged him with "Who goes there?" Receiving no answer, I repeated my question a second and a third time. Still he remained obstinately silent and immovable. I trust I am not of a rash or sanguinary disposition, but military discipline and a sense of the duty I owed to my country induced me to shut my eyes to the awful consequences and I fired my rifle. The alarm was given, the guard turned out. On being questioned, I pointed to the unfortunate object of my vigilance. The guard, preceded by the sergeant with a lanthorn, cautiously approached and upon examination found that I had lodged a bullet in the — pump.

[On] February 9, 1810, *Romeo and Juliet* was acted at the Bath theatre, Romeo "by a gentleman, being his first appearance on any stage." This gentleman, whose name was [Robert ("Romeo")] Coates, and who afterwards introduced himself to the public under the title of The Amateur of Fashion, was certainly the most extraordinary character that ever appeared before an audience. Many gentlemen have fancied themselves actors, or, that they could become so by perseverance, but no one ever continued for such a length of time to obtrude themselves upon the notice of the public in spite of the hisses and shouts of laughter and derision with which he was generally greeted. With a grave countenance and a self-satisfied demeanour he committed the grossest absurdities in action and delivery and seemed totally unconscious of the ridiculous situation in which he was placed, receiving the absurd and extravagant compliments which were paid him by those who wished to divert themselves with his egregious vanity, as tributes to his extraordinary merit. He was a well-educated man, tall and of a good figure, with much grace and elegance in his manners, an accomplished dancer and fencer, but a most unfortunate expression of countenance.

Some of the actors, bent upon fun and mischief, suggested to me, as I played the part of Tybalt to his Romeo, to signalize myself by prolonging the contest with him as long as possible, and as I was not behindhand in a stage jest, we fenced together I won't say "for an hour by the Shrewsbury clock" but till we could fence no longer, and I fell from actual exhaustion and amid the laughter and applause of the audience. Meeting him some years after in London, he recognized me, and recalling the circumstances to his recollection, and insensible to the ridicule and laughter which it had occasioned, assured me though he had played the part of Romeo several times since, the fencing scene never went off so well as it did upon that occasion.

Mr. Elliston coming down to Bath for a short engagement was induced by Mr. Lovegrove, the comedian, to witness my performance of Robert in the serious pantomime of *Raymond and Agnes* and was so well pleased with my acting that he offered for the Surrey Theatre at the liberal salary of 30s. per week. Had he proposed 15s. I think I should have taken it, so desirous was I to obtain a situation in London where I expected my abilities would be properly appreciated.

I was not deceived in my anticipation, the public have done me ample justice, and if I have not accomplished everything my vanity and ambition led me to expect, I have every reason to be satisfied with the position I have attained.

I did not part from Mr. Dimond, the manager of the Bath theatre, without regret: his kindness and amiability rendered him universally respected....

Mr. Smith as the Pirate of the Black Sea. Museum of the City of New York, Theatre and Music Collection.

Mr. Smith as Guy Fawkes. Museum of the City of New York, Theatre and Music Collection.

Mr. Smith as Rawbold the Blood Stained Saxon. Museum of the City of New York, Theatre and Music Collection.

Mr. Smith as Mammon. Collection of William W. Appleton.

Mr. Smith as Hubert in Magna Charta. Collection of William W. Appleton.

40

Mr. Smith as Obi in Three-fingered Jack. Collection of William W. Appleton.

Mr. Smith as Nigromante. Collection of William W. Appleton.

Mr. Smith as Lolonois. Collection of William W. Appleton.

West's, *Theatrical* Portraits.
№ 93.

Mr. O Smith — as Robert, in Raymond & Agness,

London, Published Feb.? 26. 1827. by W. West. at his Theatrical Print Warehouse, 57, Wych St.? Opposite the Olympic Theatre, Strand.

Mr. Smith as Robert in Raymond and Agness. Collection of William W. Appleton.

44

Mr. Smith as Three-fingered Jack. Collection of William W. Appleton.

Chapter 5th

Mr. Elliston received me very kindly, showed me over the theatre and introduced me to T.P. Cooke whom we found in front of the stage, suspended between two ladders, with his head downwards. At that time there were four pantomime clowns in the company and they were striving to outdo each other in feats of strength and agility, but Mr. Elliston soon found out that T.P. was capable of something better than playing clowns, made him stage manager, and cast him [in] several original parts which made him a favourite with the public and laid the foundation of his subsequent well-deserved reputation.

In the month of May 1810 a riot took place at the Surrey Theatre which was very inconsiderately brought about by the manager himself. Miss Giroux and Miss Taylor, two rival Columbines in the establishment, by their grace and agility were possessed of equal claims to the public patronage. In the first instance they played upon alternate nights and were supported by their numerous and respective admirers under the direction of the two leaders of the opposing parties, Messrs. Barrett and Slater, who wore the initials G. and T. in their hats, waited for the ladies at the stage door at the conclusion of the entertainment and escorted them to their homes accompanied by bands of music. Mr. Elliston then mis[takenly] argued with himself: "If these ladies are so individually attractive, what would they not prove if their talents were combined in the same piece?" so he announced them both to appear in the same pantomime and then the row began, the consequences of which soon became perceptible. That part of the audience who came for rational amusement were driven from the theatre which was very indifferently filled till half price. The first piece generally passed unnoticed, nothing was thought of or attended to but the rival Columbines. At first the opposing parties confined their demonstrations to applause, placards, handbills and ballads, but, getting angry with each other, abuse, quarrels, and at length fights, took place. The boxes were empty, the gallery who took no part in the contest were enraged at this interruption to their amusement, and a noisy and riotous pit ruled triumphant.

These disturbances continued night after night for such a length of time as to attract the notice of the magistrates. Mr. Elliston then began to perceive the folly and impolicy of his conduct in compromising the respectability of the theatre, a point which he had been previously using his utmost endeavours to establish.

He addressed the audiences every night and the performers every morning, endeavouring to convince them of what must have been sufficiently obvious to every one — his own folly and obstinacy. In July the Attorney-General applied for a Rule and a criminal information was filed against Messrs. Barrett and Slater, the leaders of the riot, and in May [of 1811], the trial took place, when the parties were convicted, but on publishing an acknowledgement of their "deep and sincere contrition for the offense they had been guilty of," and subscribing a sum of money for "the relief of the distressed Portuguese," Mr. Elliston abstained from bringing them up to receive the sentence of the court. It was my peculiar ill fortune to make my first appearance while this disturbance was going on, when nothing else was attended to, and it was not till some time afterwards that I claimed an opportunity of attracting the notice of the manager or the public.

When Mr. Elliston became lessee of the Circus, which he dignified with the title of The Surrey Theatre, he was obliged to retain the greater part of the company which had been previously engaged. Although they were good equestrians, rope dancers and tumblers, there were several among them of very questionable respectability in their private characters. (By way, I suppose, of giving them a practical hint of what their dissipated habits might lead to, Mr. Elliston used to attend the executions at Horse-monger Lane and for a time became as regular in his attendance as the sheriffs. The actors used to make up a party to witness the edifying sight of their Manager upon the scaffold dressed in solemn black with a play — no — a prayer-book in his hand.) Indeed they were a different race of beings from persons of that description at present, many of whom are gentlemen in their manners and acquirements. Mr. Elliston endeavoured to reform the laxity of discipline which prevailed among them and reduce them to submission "under the mild shadow of his government." One of the numerous proclamations he issued for the purpose commenced thus: "Whereas, several wanton outrages on the Manager's property have lately been committed, vulgarly called Sky-larking, &c."

Transported from the quiet, orderly, and respectable theatres of Edinburgh and Bath, I found myself in a new world, and for some time continued the butt of the practical jokes of the performers, till corrupted by the examples around me, I became as dissipated as the rest, and should have fallen a sacrifice, as most of them did, to drunkenness and debauchery, but that I was saved from destruction by the good sense and affection of an excellent and beloved wife – beloved for she was excellent.[2]

With his habitual inconsistency Mr. Elliston, obeying the impulse of the moment, would occasionally perform the most liberal and generous actions and with deliberation be guilty of the most contemptible meanness for which he was often reprehended by his friends, and particularly by Mr. Phipps of the Albion Insurance Office, than whom there never existed a more honourable man.

Soon after my arrival in London I began to find that 30s. a week, though a good salary in the country, would not allow me to participate in the pleasures and dissipation with which I was surrounded, and which I had not the moral courage to resist. Thinking that my exertions deserved a more liberal recompense, I applied to Mr. Elliston for an increase of salary. He assumed an air of astonishment at the proposal and after a grandiloquent discourse of half an hour in which he talked of "political economy," his "Chancellor of the Exchequer," and the fatal consequences of extravagance and dissipation of property and intellect – upon 30s. a week – he said, "Although the finances of my establishment will not allow you an increase of salary, I will give you a benefit, upon such an occasion as shall prove highly advantageous to your interests, and convince you of my desire to reward your talent as it deserves, in hopes your future conduct will justify my liberality." I felt highly gratified by this promise, but had I known him better I might have doubted a suspicious twinkling in the corner of his eye, for, as the saying is, "He would laugh with one side of his face and cry with the other."

I pacified my creditors as well as I could and waited with

---

[2]Smith's wife was named Elizabeth, surname unknown. She was his only legatee and Smith's will makes no mention of any children.

impatience for the *advantageous occasion* which was to relieve me from my embarrassments. At the latter end of the season, just before the production of the Christmas novelty, my benefit was announced on the 5th of November, Guy Fawkes Day, decidedly the worst night in the year for a benefit. The consequence was, the expenses were not in the house, and my salary was put under stoppages by the Chancellor of the Exchequer for the six following months. This placed me in a worse situation [than] before, and I was glad to avail myself of the opportunity of giving occasional assistance in the painting-room, and an appeal to Mr. Phipps at length procured me a slight increase of salary.

[On] April 4th, 1811 Mrs. Siddons played Margaret of Anjou in the tragedy of *The Earl of Warrick* for Mr. Pope's benefit at the Opera House in the Haymarket. Mr. Elliston, who played King Edward, took me with him, and I had the gratification of witnessing the performance.... There was a very great house, and behind the scenes as much crowded as the front of the theatre. Being a stranger in the theatre, I lost my way, and wandering through the numerous passages leading to the dressing-rooms, I suddenly came upon one, the door of which was open, and at the upper end of the room which was brilliantly lighted, sat Mrs. Siddons, motionless as a statue, dressed as Margaret of Anjou. She wore a kind of golden half armour, with a helmet and a plume of feathers, and a large crimson velvet robe, lined with ermine, flowed in graceful folds around her. Sir Joshua Reynolds's picture of her as the Tragic Muse in the gallery at Dulwich is doubtless a very fine picture, but no representation that I have ever seen ever equalled her noble and majestic appearance as Margaret of Anjou.

In 1811 Mr. Elliston produced "A new grand, melodramatic and moral illustration, founded on Hogarth's paintings of the Idle and Illustrious Apprentice and called Industry and Idleness." In the last scene was represented the pageant of My Lord Mayor's show and T.P. Cooke and myself rode in brass and iron armour. The suit I wore was borrowed from the Hall of the Ironmongers Company in Fenchurch Street. It weighed 97 lbs., the helmet alone being 7 lbs. weight....After a little practice, though [we] were necessarily limited and constrained, I could mount and dismount my horse without assistance, and even used to fight a combat with my friend T.P.

Cooke in the last scene of a "splendid hippodramatic romance" called *Blood will have Blood.* The greatest inconvenience I experienced was from the heat caused by the confined air, so what we read of in ancient chronicles of knights being thrown down in battle and suffocated, may be literally true....

In November 1811 Sir Claudius Hunter through Mr. Marriott made application to Mr. Elliston to allow these two suits to be worn on the occasion of his induction into Mayoralty, which Mr. Elliston very readily granted.... When we came to mount our horses...in Fleet Street a cropt-tailed hack had been provided for me...not at all capable of bearing the weight of a knight in armour, so Mr. Marriott was obliged to exert his authority and procured for me a horse belonging to a trumpeter in the horse guards with a fine flowing tail and richly caparisoned. This excited the envy of Captain D — in the City Militia...He seized the bridle of my horse and in a peremptory tone ordered me to dismount...but I felt my dignity and my armour unsuited by the demand and threatened to brain him with my gauntlet if he did not release his hold on my bridle. There is no way of knowing how far this dispute might have led to "a combat to the utterance," but the trumpets sounded *to Horse* and the valiant captain, muttering threats of vengeance, was compelled to mount the crop tailed hack and follow in my train.

On arriving at Guildhall not the slightest preparation had been made for our reception or entertainment, and for hours we were held "locked up in complete steel" without refreshment. In this state of exhaustion and fatigue we were led into the hall and I and my companion in brass placed upon pedestals 7 feet high, behind the Lord Mayor elect and his illustrious visitors. I know not how the fact became known to the Lady Mayoress of the want of attention which had been shown to us, but she most kindly sent me the leg of a pheasant. I had rather it had been the leg of an ostrich, but the favour was gratefully received. As to my brazen companion, his unthinking friends supplied him too liberally with wine, the fumes from which, caused by an empty stomach, first made him fall asleep and then very nearly fall off his pedestal. To prevent this danger to others as well as himself, he was carefully handed down from his temporary elevation and carried out of the Hall like a bale of damaged goods by four of the Lord Mayor's powdered footmen, while I covered his retreat in a very dignified manner for which I received the applause of the company.

[In] 1812-13 during the campaigns of the Duke of Wellington in Spain and Portugal, upon notice of the first success obtained, Mr. Elliston brought out a piece written for the occasion and called it *The Fall of Badajoz* in which I played the French general Philippon, and in the last scene, with the assistance of 10 supernumeraries, had to defend a fort constructed of wood and canvas, against a desperate attack made upon it by 24 supers, armed with wooden muskets and silver leather bayonets. Placed in this *highly* responsible situation, being elevated on a platform 9 feet high, I performed everything that skill and valour could effect, loading and firing without intermission, but was eventually compelled to yield up the fortress as the property man had orders not to supply me with any more gunpowder. As victory succeeded victory in rapid succession, the manager found there was not time to write and produce a new military spectacle upon every glorious occasion, so he merely altered the title and the same piece was played for Ciudad Rodrigo, San Sebastian, Salamanca &c. and I was General Philippon, Marshall Soult, or Suchet, as the change of place required. My military enthusiasm increased with every occasion for its display and at length I became so desperately courageous as to demand an additional supply of gunpowder and more supernumeraries to contend with. Mr. Elliston refused my request and remarked, "I dare say if you had been there the fortress never would have been taken." To which I inadvertently replied, "No, sir, that it never should," which, as Mr. Mathews used to say, "caused a great laugh at the time."

[By February 1812, Smith had established himself as a melodrama actor through Elliston's successful revivals of *Three-fingered Jack* and *Raymond and Agnes*. He also achieved a success as an actor in burlesque pieces, most notably in John Poole's *The Earls of Hammersmith.*]

[The title role in Poole's burlesque] was cast to Mr. Fitzwilliam and played by him for a few nights, but at the time he was suffering from a complaint in his knee and had to be carried upon the stage in a chair to perform the character. When he was no longer capable of the exertion Mr. T.P. Cooke was obliged to undertake the part. At that time I was walking at the head of a procession in the same piece. T.P. was the only [one in the] theatre to perceive my talent for

burlesque and very good naturedly recommended me to perform
the character. I was successful in the representation and when the
piece was afterward transplanted to the Olympic, Mr. Mathews came
several nights to see it and spoke very highly of the performance.

In 1813 Mr. Elliston, having purchased the Olympic Theatre in
Wynch Street, Drury Lane, of Mr. Astley for £3,000, it was announced
to open on Monday, April 13 under the title of "The little Drury
Lane Theatre," but the patentees of the Theatre Royal felt their
dignity so hurt by this assumption that they appealed to the Lord
Chamberlain who closed the theatre for a short time till it had
undergone a purgation for the offence when it was reopened under
the old title of The Olympic. Mr. Kean being engaged by Mr.
Elliston, as stage manager and actor, was to have made his first
appearance in the character of Mandeville in the melodrama of *The
False Friend*, but a previous engagement with Drury Lane prevented
him. The matter was not settled without some difficulty, and in
consequence of the absence of Mr. Kean, I was sent over from the
Surrey to play the part of Mandeville, Mr. H. Wallack was engaged
to play the Captain of Banditti and Mr. Russell assumed the situation
of stage manager.

There was at this time living in the Rules of the King's Bench an
officer of rank, considerably indebted to my deceased father, who
had become answerable for several bills he had left unpaid during
his visit to Bath. As my mother was left very indifferently provided
for, except [for] a trifling annuity from the Bath Theatrical Fund, I
waited upon this gentleman who received me very kindly and
invited me to dine with him. After dinner, over our wine, I stated
the purpose of my visit, when I perceived a visible change in his
countenance and manner. However, he was very profuse in his
acknowledgement, professed his willingness to repay my mother,
the obligations he had been under to my father, regretted that it was
not in his power at present, and dismissed me with assurances of
regard and "all that sort of thing, and everything else in the world!"
as [Mr.] Mathews used to say. From that time it unfortunately
happened that he was never at home when I called and returned no
answer to my numerous applications by letter. At length, offended
by my pertinacity, he caused me to be drawn for the militia, and as I
was not exempt from the conscription and could not afford a substitute,

Mr. Elliston sent me down to Birmingham to produce *The Miller and His Men, Aladdin,* and *The Wood Demon.* Mr. Mathews, with that kind and liberal feeling which influenced all his actions, had not forgotten my performance in the *Earls of Hammersmith* and strongly recommended me to Mr. Morris of the Haymarket who made me a very liberal offer of an engagement, but I was under a previous article with Mr. Elliston and too *generally useful* to be spared by him, so I lost an opportunity which under the patronage of Mr. Mathews might have turned to my advantage. As I superintended the production of the melodramas above mentioned, and came from a theatre where I had been received in that line of business, my *amour propre* was highly offended when the stage manager, taking advantage of his situation, appropriated the principal characters in the pieces to himself and cast me in inferior parts. After some altercation with Mr. Elliston on the subject, as he did not seem inclined to do me justice, I tendered my resignation which to my surprise and mortification he accepted.

In the month of November [1813] I left Birmingham to join the company of Messrs. Anderson and Faulkner at South Shields. Being very indifferently provided with the *material* for such a journey, my wife and myself took our passage in a collier in ballast from London and entered the Tyne River with above 200 sail who had been wind bound in Yarmouth Roads for several weeks. With this company I remained till [1815] when I accepted the situation of stage manager with Mr. Vickers at the Royalty Theatre, Wellclose Square. Here I met with Clarkson Stanfield, since so justly celebrated as one of our first English artists. He had just returned from a voyage to India and was engaged as scene painter at the Royalty. We lodged together in the house of a painter and glazier in Cannon Street Road. When he returned from the theatre of an evening he used to paint and sketch, and the landlord observing some of Stanfield's productions exclaimed, "Ah! I do something in that way myself," and going down to the shop he returned and exhibited with great self-gratification *a red bow and a blue mangle.*

Mr. Vickers's affairs becoming deranged and the theatre falling into other hands, I left and [made] my first appearance at Covent Garden in the character of Othello. "What?" I think I hear the reader exclaim. "Othello!" Even so — in the grand pageant on the [bi-] centenary of Shakespeare's [death.]

Taking advantage of my introduction to Covent Garden, I witnessed John Kemble's performance of all his most celebrated characters previous to his retirement 23rd June 1817. He was unequalled in the representation of characters of majesty and grandeur, as Cato, King John, Cardinal Wolsey — not that he wanted fire and spirit when the occasion required — witness his awful denunciations in *King Lear*, his impatient and insulted pride in *Coriolanus*, his sudden bursts of passion as Hotspur — these were finely contrasted with the most affecting touches of nature as the philosophic Prince of Denmark, the temperate Brutus, and the philanthropic Penruddock. It was affecting to see him after leaving the stage where he had exerted himself in portraying his most powerful passions with an appearance of manly vigour, behind the scenes supported by an attendant, bending beneath infirmity and oppressed with asthma.

I made my re-appearance at the Surrey Theatre under the management of Mr. Thomas Dibdin Easter Monday 1817 and May 12th was produced the burlesque of *Don Giovanni, or, the Spectre on Horseback*. The part of Don Guzman the Commandant was originally intended for another actor in the theatre, but he was so dissipated and inattentive that Mr. Dibdin became alarmed for the success of his piece and looked through the company to find a substitute.

Consulting Fitzwilliam on the subject, he remembered my success in the *Earls of Hammersmith* and recommended me to Mr. Dibdin's notice. He sent for me and questioned me as to my capability for the part — of which no one ought to have been a better judge than himself — whether I thought I should be able to get through the character — if he should divide it, so that someone else might play Don Guzman and me the ghost? I felt severely mortified by these doubts of my capability, but I knew what I could do with the part and merely said that if he pleased I would do the best I could with the character as it stood, if he thought proper to entrust me with it. Afterwards he certainly did me the justice to acknowledge that my performance of Don Guzman contributed very materially to the success of the piece, which ran for rather more than 100 successive nights and was frequently played afterwards.

I believe there are very few actors who have been indebted to the patronage or discernment of managers for their eminence in the profession. When established talent attracts their notice they are anxious to obtain it, and offer most liberal terms to secure it for themselves: perhaps to deprive some rival theatre of a source of attraction, then, not being able to make an advantageous use of that which they have paid an extravagant price for, they lay the actor upon the shelf and having destroyed his popularity — for an actor can be no longer popular than while he is before the audience — they discharge him at the end of his engagement.

While managers are thus in search of talent abroad, they neglect the indications of it in their own theatres, for I do not believe there is any actor, however inferior his situation may be, but possesses at least a share of merit in some particular or the other, and one would think that it would be the duty as well as the interest of the manager to place it in a favourable point of view.

No one possessed this tact in a superior degree than Mr. Dibdin who wrote for his actors and introduced several to the public notice who would otherwise have remained in obscurity. I have known him after a piece had been written and rehearsed, recollect that some actor had been omitted in the cast, and sitting down he would write a character [who] would prove as effective as any other in the piece. This talent, added to the method and regularity with which the business of the theatre was conducted, the superior taste and judgment which directed the production of the pieces, offered to the public notice several as perfect representations as were ever seen on any stage. Let me instance *The Heart of Midlothian, The Fate of Calais, Constantine and Valeria,* and *The Siege of Troy.*

It has often excited the surprise and even the censure of those who were not aware of the causes which led to Mr. Dibdin's failure at the Surrey Theatre that after the extraordinary success which attended the production of the most popular pieces he should have been compelled to make such frequent appeals to the public. Everything in the theatre during his management was conducted with the greatest regard to economy and regularity. He was not a man of expensive habits, and his greatest enjoyment seemed to be in writing for his actors and directing the business of the stage. According to the statement in his *Memoirs* [London: Colburn, 1827, vol. II, p. 112] which I know to be literally correct, when he took the Surrey Theatre, "The whole of the interior of the theatre required substantial repair: there was not a scene, nor a frame to hang one on: the dressing-places, and even the stairs, had been pulled down by the last tenant (Mr. Dunn, who had removed to the Coburg everything that was movable). There was not a chandelier nor a candlestick: the estimate of what it was to cost me to supply these deficiencies was stated by respectable men at about £2,000 — it cost me four, before I could draw up the curtain."

This money being borrowed upon extravagant interest involved Mr. Dibdin in a series of difficulties which all his talent and indefatigable industry could never overcome, and after vainly struggling against the tide of misfortune he was compelled in [1822] to dismiss his company and resign the theatre into other hands. I am sure it was not among the least of his regrets that of parting with those with whom he had been so long associated.

The Coburg Theatre which opened under the management of Mr. Glossop [on May 11, 1818] proved a powerful rival to the Surrey. The means of lavish expense possessed by Mr. Glossop completely overpowered all Mr. Dibdin's attempts at competition and for some time monopolized the patronage of the public. The pieces were produced by Mr. Barrymore on a most extraordinary scale of magnificence and splendour. Messrs. Stanfield and Roberts painted the scenery and the company comprised Mr. Barrymore Senr., Mr. Huntley, Mr. and Mrs. Stanley, Mr. and Mrs. Davidge, Mr. Beverly, Sloman and Mrs. Barrymore, an actress whose talent would have been an acquisition to any theatre.

[From 1818-21, O. Smith was associated with a number of theatres. He performed for Glossop at the Coburg, and for Mr. Ray at the Royalty Theatre in 1819. Subsequently he returned to the Coburg Theatre, and on June 7th, 1821, made his first appearance at Drury Lane, under Elliston's management, as Malcolm in *The Falls of Clyde*. His reminiscences of this period of his life are extremely fragmentary and his association with Elliston is barely mentioned. He also appeared at provincial theatres and tells of the following incident that occurred in Birmingham in 1823.]

In the course of the season Power played for a few nights and when his benefit was announced by way of extra-ordinary attraction and for that night only he advertised the melodrama of *Frankenstein* without the least consideration how it was to be done without music, scenery, or dresses. Those who have seen *Frankenstein* are, of course, aware that the dress of the Monster is a very peculiar one, being a close fitting stocking dress and a Grecian tunic of the same grey colour. Neither Mr. Bunn nor Mr. Power would go to the expense of procuring a dress of this description, and I was left to my own resources which could find no better substitute than a comfortable surtout, pantaloons, and boots. At rehearsal the scenery was selected from such as the theatre afforded, and according to a theatrical saying, "If you can't snow white, you must snow brown."[3] When we

---

[3]For a discussion of this aphorism, see Percy Fitzgerald, *The World Behind the Scenes* (London: Chatto and Windus, 1881), pp. 62 – 63.

came to the last scene where Frankenstein and the Monster are to be destroyed by an avalanche, it was necessary to hold a consultation with the Master Carpenter. The manager, who was a person not to be conquered by difficulties of any sort, stated that an avalanche was absolutely necessary to conclude this piece. The Master Carpenter replied that they had not got such a thing in the house, but they had got a [property] elephant. "The very thing," replied the Manager. "Whitewash him. Fill his belly with paper snow. Hang him up in the flies and when you hear a second pistol shot let go — I'll answer for the effect."

In the last scene it was intended that Frankenstein and the Monster should be elevated on a platform in the center of the stage, and when a pistol was fired by Frankenstein the avalanche was to have fallen amid a shower of snow and concealed them from the audience. Fortunately, as it happened, before we reached our elevation a pistol was fired behind the scenes, when the Master Carpenter being overanxious for the success of the experiment let go — when down came the elephant with a tremendous crash, knocked down the platform and scenery and came rolling down the stage to the footlights where it ran some danger of being roasted till it was dragged off the stage by the green-coat men, and the curtain dropped upon Frankenstein amid the laughter and applause of a good natured audience.

[In the course of this period Weber's *Der Freischütz* had its London premiere under Elliston's management at Drury Lane on November 10th 1824.]

The fate of this opera was very singular. It was produced in Germany with great success, but Sir George Smart [the conductor] told me that Weber, the composer, could not bear to hear the opera mentioned. A compliment upon it displeased him. It seems the score was parted with to discharge an old debt of £30 which was the only profit he ever derived from it. After having been rejected by both the theatres, Covent Garden and Drury Lane, it subsequently became one of the most favorite and attractive pieces ever known and more improved the taste of the public than any other production for the previous twenty years. Yet the overture when first attempted to be played at an oratorio at Drury Lane was so much disapproved of by the audience that they would not hear it to a conclusion and the director was obliged to substitute the Overture to *Anacreon*. At length the wild romantic story, the terrific incidents, picturesque scenery, beautiful airs and original melodies which pervaded the opera, offered such a pleasing variety that it deservedly became a most popular and fashionable entertainment. There were no less than seven alterations and adaptations produced in London.

This opera was likewise the means of introducing to the public notice several performers whose merits were not so generally known or appreciated as they ought to have been, particularly Mr. Horn, Mr. Phillips, Miss Paton, [and] Miss Graddon.

The part of Zamiel likewise commenced the list of my infernal triumphs and procured for me the following notice in a monthly publication where my performance was considered as "a most extraordinary conception and powerful delineation of character.... Mr. O. Smith's Devil is as much superior to his infernal rivals as Milton's Satan is superior to the vulgar horned and tailed Devils of Tasso." [The following device appears without explanation in Smith's manuscript.]

O. Smith

O ut of a chasm blazing with red fire
S ee great O Smith arise, to chill with fright:
M aking night hideous, and the young desire
I n arms maternal to exclude the sight.
T o thee thou artist actor praise is due
H erein our Martin and our Wilkie too.[4]

In June 1829 performing the part of Zamiel with Mr. Schutz's German company at Covent Garden Theatre, though I only went through the pantomime business of the character and had nothing to say, the papers the next morning complimented me on my manner of speaking the German language. "The Devil was an Englishman, Mr. O. Smith, whose cavernous tones lent terrors to the original German."

---

[4]John Martin, the apocalyptic painter, and David Wilkie whose paintings were often reproduced as tableaux on the Victorian stage.

Chapter 7th

[On July 2, 1827, O. Smith appeared at the English Opera House for the first time. He was playing the role of Githian, a maniac, in Richard Peake's *The Cornish Miners*. We are told that he excelled in a scene where he visits the grave of his lost child and covers it with flowers. He also supervised the melodramatic action. During the same season he was also appearing as the unnamed Monster in Peake's *Presumption, or, The Fate of Frankenstein*, a role which had originally been created by T.P. Cooke. It was during this engagement that he had his first encounter with the eccentric comedian, Charles Mathews.]

In one of my visits to Gravesend I procured a bill describing the particulars of the entertainments provided at an annual fair held at Northfleet. Mr. Mathews at that time was nightly singing "The Country Fair," and knowing that he set a value on anything rare or eccentric, I determined to make use of this bill as a means of introduction to his acquaintance, and at the same time furnish me with an opportunity of thanking him for the favourable opinion he had been pleased to express of my abilities.

Meeting him on the stage previous to rehearsal, I made my best bow, and presenting him with the bill for his acceptance, requested, if he thought it worthy of preservation, that it might be added to his collection of oddities. He thanked me, I thought rather coldly, and said he had no doubt he might borrow a hint from it to suit his purpose. In the evening Mr. Peake informed me that Mr. Mathews had expressed himself as follows: "This morning, sir, upon my entrance into the theatre I was accosted by a gentleman who requested my *acceptance of a bill*. This rather startled me, but I was relieved from my alarm when I found it was a bill of a fair, which I was requested to add to my collection. Now, sir, experience has taught me to be very cautious in my acceptance of trifling presents from strangers, as they have generally turned out to be very troublesome and expensive in the end. One person will present me with a cinder from Herculaneum and the next day request me to cash a bill for him of doubtful acceptance. Another will offer me a pair of brass knee buckles worn by Queen Anne and invites himself to dine with me and brings a party of friends with him under pretence of seeing my collection. Not knowing Mr. O. Smith in his private character, nor conceiving that he could look so like a gentleman, though I have often admired his talent on the stage, where he generally looks like anything else, I am afraid I received his present rather coolly, for which I beg you will present my apologies to him and say I shall be most happy in forming his acquaintance." Shortly after I had the pleasure of an introduction to Mr. Mathews, when he gave me the following certificate of my private respectability.

I am happy to have it in my power to express my perfect belief that Mr. Smith is a most respectable character in private life though a great ruffian on the stage. C. Mathews, Theatre Royal English Opera House, August 21st, 1827.

[In the autumn, on October 16, 1827, Smith made his Covent Garden debut as the Black Huntsman in *Der Freischütz*. He also appeared there in the title role of *The Bottle Imp*. The following summer he returned to the English Opera House.]

During the English Opera Season [in] 1828 I addressed the following letter to Mr. Arnold, requesting an increase in salary. It was inserted in one or two of the daily papers and some of my friends flattered me so far as to say that it was not my writing, by which I suppose they meant that it was either too good or not good enough to have been written by me. Subsequently, however, the original letter produced £5 5s. at the sale of Mr. Thomas Hill's library and papers.

August 1828

Sir,

For some months past I have made most extraordinary efforts to suppress the warmth of my feelings, but find it impossible to remain any longer silent upon a subject which has proved detrimental to my interests, injurious to my health, and destructive to my peace of mind. As the remedy for my grievances remains in your hands, I confidently rely upon your well known liberality and kindness of disposition to afford me relief from my present unparalleled state of suffering. During the last five or six years of my professional career, the managers of the London theatres have deemed it essential to their interests that I should play nothing but demons, devils, monsters and assassins, and the audience, by the apparent gratification with which they have witnessed my transmigrations have confirmed the managers in their opinions, so that I begin almost to doubt my own identity. This unfortunate celebrity has, in the first place, deprived me of all social intercourse. I find myself banished from all respectable society. What man will receive the Devil upon friendly terms or introduce a demon into his family circle? My infernal reputation follows me everywhere. The other evening a well meaning but thoughtless friend of mine introduced me in a party as the Devil in *Der Freischütz*. I immediately perceived the company regard me with half-averted and suspicious looks, so I took the first opportunity to vanish with as small a smell of sulphur as possible. But even these mortifications I could submit to, being naturally of a reserved and saturnine — not satanic — disposition, but that my pecuniary interests suffer with my feelings. The last time I attempted a benefit, I burnt my fingers. People would as soon think of purchasing a turnpike ticket for Pandemonium as a ticket for the Devil's benefit. No country manager will engage me unless I agree to find my own fireworks and travel with at least 10 lbs. of red fire in my carpet bag.

My health has likewise suffered very materially from the mephitic vapours or red, blue and green fire with which I am continually surrounded. The showers of sparks to which I am nightly exposed have very nearly burnt all the hair off my head, and an alarming cough has settled upon my lungs from the unnatural atmosphere I am compelled to breath, so that I may say with Grimbald in Dryden [and Garrick's] *Arthur and Emmeline*

> I had a voice in Heav'n ere sulphurous steams
> Had damp'd it into hoarseness. [II, i]

In short, sir, I must request that you will sometimes allow me to appear before the public in my own natural shape in order to satisfy them of my identity with something human, and, as I have literally *gone through fire* to serve you, you will take my exertions into consideration and reward them in an adequate manner or I shall shortly be qualified to succeed M. [Xavier] Chabert, the Fire King, and be compelled to exhibit myself as an interesting specimen of anti combustion, which perhaps you will say would be jumping out of the frying pan into the fire. Will you likewise be pleased to warn the managers in town and country that I cannot afford to play the Devil any longer upon the same terms as at present, and that it will be impossible for me in the future to drag all or any of the stage libertines by the hair of their heads to the infernal regions unless I shall be more liberally remunerated for my exertions, since all the life insurance offices have declared my life, in consequence of the line of business I play, *doubly hazardous!* I trust you will excuse the warmth of the expressions I have made use of, but I could no longer smother the pent-up flame that glowed within my breast, and fired with the subject, have hazarded this explosion of my feelings to prevent spontaneous combustion since I can no longer endure this Hell upon Earth. I am,

Warmly yours,

O. Smith.

[Despite his plea, Smith continued to play demonic villains, but the season at Covent Garden was briefly interrupted in November, 1828, by a curious accident.]

Covent Garden was announced to be closed for one week, for the ostensible purpose of removing the gas [jets] from the Dress Circle of the Boxes, and the passages and lobbies of the theatre, but in reality to arrange the affairs of the proprietors which had fallen into a state of difficulty and disorder.

Thursday the 18th at ½ past 12 o'clock [in the] morning as I was reading the papers at Harris's in Bow Street, I was alarmed by a tremendous explosion in Covent Garden Theatre, and hurrying to the spot, soon learnt the cause of the alarm so visible in every countenance. For some time past the offensive smell arising from the gas, which had been prepared on the premises, was supposed to have deterred many persons from visiting the theatre, and the proprietors had determined to remove the cause of complaint, and for this purpose had closed the theatre for a week to make the necessary alterations. During the temporary absence of the superintendent, one of the unfortunate sufferers, from his own imprudence, perforated a small hole in the gasometer, with a view of burning out the offensive gas, and applied a lighted candle to the orifice, when the foul vapour ignited, and a tremendous explosion took place. Volumes of smoke instantly issued from the windows of the theatre, and the alarm being given, and 8 or 10 engines were quickly on the spot, and by quenching the flames prevented the destruction of the theatre. Two men of the names of Douglas and Fennell were suffocated in the passages by the horrid effluvia and three were conveyed to the hospital in a deplorable condition, where two of them afterwards died.

The performers, in the meantime, with the consent of the proprietors and the sanction of the Lord Chamberlain, performed at the Theatre Royal English Opera House, and Mr. Kean in the most kind and liberal manner volunteered his gratuitous services. On Saturday November 29th Mr. Kean was presented with an elegant silver snuff box by the performers of Covent Garden Theatre for his gratuitous services for four nights at the [Theatre Royal English Opera House] in an attempt to pay for the minor salaries of the Covent Garden company during the vacation.

Having received a friendly hint that there was an opening for me at the Adelphi Theatre I waited upon Mr. Yates and soon came to terms with him. I made my first appearance at the Adelphi October 12th 1829 in the pantomime of [Obi, or] Three-fingered Jack in which Mr. Yates condescended to play the part of Rosa.

[In all likelihood the friendly hint came from Charles Mathews, co-manager of the Adelphi with Frederick Yates. T.P. Cooke, Sinclair, and Miss Graddon had left the Adelphi company and were replaced by Smith, John Reeve, and Mrs. Fitzwilliam. Smith took over Cooke's roles and on December 3rd created a new role as Hafed, the Fire Fiend, in the sensation of the season, The Elephant of Siam.]

Ever on the search after novelty, in 1829 Mr. Yates engaged an elephant of extraordinary sagacity and docility which he introduced to the public notice [on] December 3rd with a whimsical address written by Mr. Beazley and spoken by Mr. Yates in the character of a Beef-eater. This extraordinary animal attracted numerous visitors to the Adelphi, among others the Duchess of Kent and the Princess Victoria, her present majesty, honoured the Adelphi with a visit December 10th. After the performance the royal party came behind the scenes and the Princess, without the slightest fear or hesitation, gave the elephant some sugar from her little hand, which the animal received and swallowed in a very decorous manner.

After it had proved sufficiently attractive at the Adelphi, Mr. Yates made engagements for it in America, and, I believe, profited greatly by the speculation. The sagacity of this animal was extraordinary and displayed itself upon the voyage in a singular manner. Mr. Yates received advices from New York, dated January 1, 1831, which informed him of the safe arrival of Mademoiselle D'Jeck after a stormy passage of eight weeks, during which they were driven upwards of 2,000 miles out of their course.

At one time the vessel having shipped a heavy sea, the elephant was washed completely out of the house erected for her accommodation upon deck. As she lay wallowing in the lee scuppers, she twisted her trunk around the ropes and chains which secured her stable to the deck and held on till the vessel righted, and assistance being afforded her she was enabled to regain her former position.

Upon her arrival in New York she was placed in a coach-house, as temporary lodging for the night, and amused herself by putting her trunk into carriage windows and picking out the whole of the lining and stuffing as neatly as an upholsterer could have done.

At the theatre, when the servants were gone to dinner, she opened the door of her den and walked upon the stage where a scene happened to be lying down for the purpose of being primed, that is, white-washed. Upsetting the pail of whiting and size, she took the large brush in her trunk and after smearing the scene all over, began painting herself till the arrival of the keeper put an end to her artistic propensities.

Amongst the numerous visitors a party of native Indians came to see her, and though they must have been greatly astonished at her bulk and docility, with their habitual self-command they forbore to express any surprise. A lithographic likeness having been published was presented to them, which seemed to puzzle them strangely how so large an animal could be contained in so small a space. After a consultation amongst themselves, the chief asked for a sheet of paper which he placed against the elephant and rubbing it hard seemed disappointed that he could not procure an impression.

Poor Mademoiselle D'Jeck was destroyed at Geneva June, 1837. Becoming infuriated [sic], her keepers were obliged to confine her in the ditch or fosse of the city, where all attempts to pacify her and restore her to reason having failed, they were at last compelled to destroy her with cannon shot. By a singular coincidence this was the second elephant that had gone mad and been destroyed, in the same place, and in the same manner, within 17 years.

Chapter 8th

On Tuesday [February 16, 1830] about one o'clock in the morning I was awakened by the cry of "Fire!", the clank of fire-engines and the confused murmur of the mob. Looking out of the front-room window — I then resided in Brydges Street — I perceived an immense body of smoke and flame rising above the houses in Exeter Street. The neighborhood was soon filled with people, and the effect of the glare of light upon them and the surrounding buildings was terrifically grand.

One is so apt to be deceived in the direction of a fire that at first I had some doubts as to where it could be: but the increasing glow of light and heat soon convinced me that it could be no other than the English Opera House. Every assistance was afforded by the fire engineers belonging to the different companies, but the combustible nature of the materials in the building defied every attempt to preserve it, till at length the roof deprived of its supports fell in with a tremendous crash and for some moments all was involved in smoke and darkness. Upon this clearing off, the appearance of the burning ruins was magnificent. The large area of the theatre was one bright body of fire, which arose in a column of flame almost too brilliant to look upon, 30 or 40 feet above the neighboring buildings, till having exhausted its fury, about five o'clock, it partially subsided and by seven was totally subdued. The theatre [had] been totally destroyed with its valuable library of books and music, wardrobe, stock of scenery, a magnificent orrery, and 15 adjoining houses completely gutted. The damage was estimated at not less than £60,000.

[On] Monday July 14th, 1834 the new Lyceum and English Opera House opened for the season with "God Save the King" sung by the whole company and [an] address spoken by Mr. Searle, the stage manager: *The Yeoman's Daughter, Call Again Tomorrow,* and *Amateurs and Actors.* The house was not so well filled as might have been expected owing to unreasonable fears with regard to the safety of the building, the heat of the weather, and unfinished state of the theatre, the unpleasant smell from gas newly laid on, paint and plastering not thoroughly dry, and the change in the bill of the performance — however, those who did attend seemed highly gratified with the elegance and splendor of the new theatre. They welcomed their old favorites with applause and departed to all appearance satisfied that the promises so long held out to them had been amply fulfilled. . . .

[Smith discusses the death of Charles Mathews, an actor he admired. "His was not the mere mimicry of voice and manner — he possessed a peculiar power of copying the minds of persons he imitated . . . a copious store of anecdote, the quickest perception possible of the ridiculous, [and] an unequalled talent for singing comic songs of a school which he himself originated, in which speaking is combined with singing. . . ." Smith then discusses the death of John Reeve who died on January 24, 1838, at the age of 39.]

John Reeve possessed more natural requisites for the stage than any actor I ever knew. Though rather stout for so young a man, he possessed great ease and agility in his movements, had rather a handsome countenance capable of the most varied expression, a voice of most excellent quality and compass, an original conception of character, great natural humor, and a strong perception of the ridiculous, irresistible in its effects upon the audience and even upon the actors themselves. With all these valuable qualifications, he had no fixed principles of action, satisfied with the consciousness of what he might do, he omitted to do that which he ought to have done. Full of whim and drollery, depending on the impulse of the moment, for it was quite uncertain one moment what he would do or say the next, he never cared to sustain a character. He knew he could always create mirth, and aware of that power he continually sacrificed propriety to a laugh, but he had naturally higher qualifications and could occasionally identify himself with the object of representation, witness his sketches of character in *Bachelor's Torments*, his church-warden in *The Forgery*, Magog in *The Wreck Ashore*, Zane Kabobs in *The Evil Eye*, and Jack Rag in *The Climbing Boy*.

He was the pet child of the Adelphi and they spoiled him, for he failed at Covent Garden and the Haymarket. Acted upon by circumstances, he was either assiduous or indolent, generous or suspicious, captious or friendly, peevish or humerous, "every thing by turns and nothing long." In the morning when cool and collected, kind, gentlemanly and agreeable, in the evening, when excited, insolent, sullen, and overbearing. Impatient of contradiction and entertaining a high opinion of his literary acquirements, in occasional arguments with his brother actors he would assume a dictatorial manner and lard his conversation with familiar phrases in Latin or French, which silenced if it did not convince them, then he would crown his triumph with some absurdity which provoked their laughter and applause. No man had a larger circle of acquaintances — no man had fewer friends, for those who made the gravest faces at his excesses on the stage were among the first to encourage those excesses when off. He sunk at last, the victim of what is absurdly called good fellowship. "I could well wish courtesy would invent some other custom of entertainment."

[Smith concludes his autobiography with a brief account of Frederick Yates who, after the death of Charles Mathews, for a brief period turned over the management of the Adelphi to Charles James Mathews. The latter, however, soon abandoned management, and Yates remained sole manager of the Adelphi until his death in 1842.]

[He] fulfilled his trust to the satisfaction of everyone under his management and the gratification of the public by his indefatigable exertions in the production of a continued succession of novelty aided by the admirable acting of Mrs. Yates, himself, and a small but talented company. It were a hopeless task to attempt to enumerate all the successful pieces he produced, but *Victorine, The Wreck Ashore, Agnes D'Aubin, Heart of London, The Forgery, Henriette, Isabel,* [and] *The Duchess de Vaubaliere* will always [be] associated with the recollection of Mr. Yate's management of the Adelphi.

Notwithstanding the reputation he had acquired when he became a manager, he found it to be to his interest to let others act as well as himself, being superior to the egregious folly of sacrificing his own interest and the feelings of others to the gratification of his professional vanity. After reading a piece to the company — and an admirable reader he was — he threw down the parts upon the table, always reserving an inferior part for himself, to which he gave a rank and consequence which it would not possess in the hands of anyone else. As for the rest, there could be no mistake, there were 9 [other] parts and 9 actors to play them — Mr. and Mrs. Yates, John Reeve, Buckstone, O. Smith and Hemming, Mrs. Fitzwilliam, Miss Ap John, Mrs. F. Matthews, and Miss Daly. So each of us took that up which properly belonged to [him.] Herein lay the secret of the success of the Adelphi. Every actor was furnished with a character suited to his peculiar talent, nor was anyone sacrificed to the selfish vanity or ambition of another, altogether forming a combination of talent which established the theatre in the estimation of the public and will cause many of the pieces acted there to be long remembered for their completeness in effect and their display of histrionic ability.

At this theatre I remained with the exception of two seasons at the Haymarket till the year [1854]. "And here," as Robinson Crusoe says, "resolving to harrass myself no more, I am preparing for a long journey, having lived [for sixty-eight] years a life of infinite variety, and learned sufficiently to know the value of retirement and the blessing of ending our days in peace."[5]

---

[5]This closing paragraph appeared elsewhere in the manuscript but evidently as a late addition. Smith died on February 1, 1855 at the age of sixty-nine.

INDEX